GLOBETROTTER

ITALIAN
In Your Pocket

GLOBETROTTER™

First edition published in 2004
by New Holland Publishers Ltd
London • Cape Town • Sydney • Auckland
10 9 8 7 6 5 4 3

website:
www.newhollandpublishers.com

Garfield House, 86 Edgware Road
London W2 2EA
United Kingdom

80 McKenzie Street
Cape Town 8001
South Africa

14 Aquatic Drive
Frenchs Forest, NSW 2086
Australia

218 Lake Road
Northcote, Auckland
New Zealand

ISBN 1 84330 637 9

Publishing Manager (UK): Simon Pooley
Publishing Manager (SA): Thea Grobbelaar
Designer: Lellyn Creamer
Illustrator: Marisa Galloway
Editor: Thea Grobbelaar
Translator: Gillian Bugg
Proofreader: Silvana Sabbatino

Reproduction by Resolution, Cape Town
Printed and bound in India by
Replika Press (Pvt) Ltd

Cover photograph: *Alfresco dining in Venice, Italy.*

CONTENTS

PHRASE BOOK

Introduction 4
How to use this book 6
Pronunciation 8
Grammar 14
Basics 22
Transport 30
Accommodation 40
Eating and Drinking 48
Money and Shopping 58
Activities 64
Health and Safety 70
Etiquette 76
Holidays and Festivals 84

DICTIONARY

English - Italian 88
Italian - English 140

INTRODUCTION

This PHRASE BOOK is thematically colour-coded for easy use and is organized according to the situation you're most likely to be in when you need it. The fairly comprehensive DICTIONARY section consists of two parts – English/Italian and Italian/English.

To make speaking Italian easy, we encourage our readers to memorize some general PRONUNCIATION rules (*see* page 8). After you have familiarized yourself with the basic tools of the language and the rudiments of Italian GRAMMAR (*see* page 14), all you need to do is turn to the appropriate section of the phrase book and find the words you need to make yourself understood. If the selection is not exactly what you're looking for, consult the dictionary for other options.

Just to get you started, here are some Italian expressions you might have heard, read or used at some time: *arrivederci*, *ciao*, *presto*, *buon giorno*, *grazie*, *si*, *crescendo*, *amore*. Even if you are unfamiliar with these words and would rather not try to say them out loud, just remain confident, follow our

easy advice and practise a little, and you will soon master useful phrases for everyday life. Speak slowly and enunciate carefully and your counterpart is likely to follow suit.

Some Italian words are pronounced a little differently from their English equivalents (e.g. zero - *dzeh-roh)*, or else changed just slightly (monument - *monumento*), though their meanings remain clear. Nowadays many English terms are used in Italian, especially in business, sport and leisure activities, so everyone will know what you mean when you say things like 'laptop', 'golf' and 'tennis'.

A section on HOLIDAYS AND FESTIVALS (*see* page 82) provides some background knowledge so that you know what you're celebrating and why. There's no better way to learn a language than joining in some of the enjoyment!

The brief section on manners, mannerisms and ETIQUETTE (*see* page 76) can help you make sense of the people around you. Make an effort to view your host country and its people tolerantly - that way you will be open to the new experience and able to enjoy it.

HOW TO USE THIS BOOK

Learning a new language can be a wonderful but frightening experience. It is not the object of this book to teach you perfect Italian, but rather to equip you with just enough knowledge for a successful holiday or business trip. Luckily you are unlikely to be criticized on your grammatical correctness when merely asking for directions. The most important thing is to make yourself understood. To this end a brief section on grammar and a guide to pronunciation have been included in this book. There is, however, no substitute for listening to native speakers.

Before you leave, it might be a good idea to familiarize yourself with the sections on Pronunciation, Grammar and Etiquette. This can easily be done en route to your destination. You will also benefit from memorizing a few important phrases before you go.

The sections of the Phrase Book are arranged by topic for quick reference. Simply go to the contents list (*see* page 3) to find the topic you need. The Dictionary section (*see* page 88) goes both ways, helping you to understand and be understood.

Abbreviations have been used in those instances where one English word could be interpreted as more than one part of speech, e.g. 'smoke' (a noun, the substance coming from a fire) and 'smoke' (a verb, what one would do with a cigarette). Here is a list of these and some other abbreviations used in this book:

vb	verb
n	noun
adj	adjective
adv	adverb
prep	preposition
pol	polite
fam	familiar (informal)
elec	electric/al
med	medical
anat	anatomy
rel	religion

The gender and number of Italian nouns have been specified as follows:

m	masculine
f	feminine
pl	plural

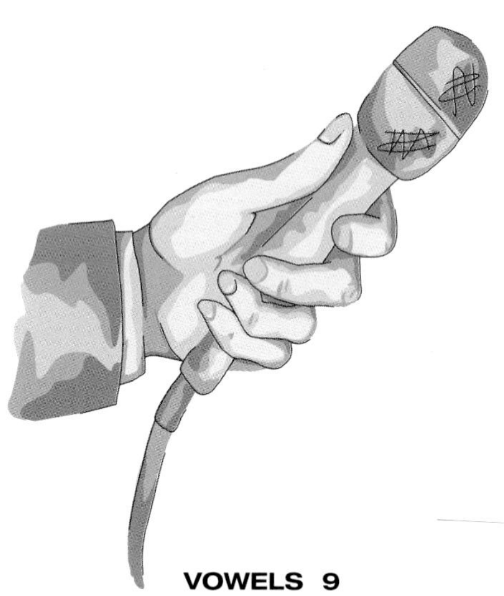

VOWELS 9
VOCALI 9

CONSONANTS 10
CONSONANTI 10

GENERAL 12
GENERALE 12

Italian is a Romance language which evolved from Latin. The pronunciation of an Italian word is very similar to the way it is written. The stress in Italian usually falls on the second-last syllable (e.g. *casa*, *ragazzo*, *matita*). If the stress is on the last syllable, the Italian word has a written grave accent (e.g. *città*, *verità*).

The Italian alphabet is the same as the English alphabet, but the letters **j**, **k**, **x**, **y** and **w** are found only in foreign words.

VOWELS

VOCALI

The Italian vowels are **a**, **e**, **i**, **o** and **u**. Each vowel has only one sound, but **o** and **e** can be open or closed according to their position:

- **a** – pronounced like the **a** in car – *sala (sah-lah)* – hall; but it is shorter in Italian – *la (lah)* – the
- **e** – pronounced like the **ai** in **said** – *letto (leht-toh)* – bed; or like the **e** in **lemon** – *mela (meh-lah)* – apple
- **i** – pronounced like the **ee** in **meet** – *vino (vee-noh)* – wine

- **o** - pronounced like the **o** in n**o**t - *posta (pos-tah)* - post; or like the **o** in alm**o**st - *sono (soh-noh)* - I am
- **u** - pronounced like the **oo** in m**oo**n - *cura (koo-rah)* - cure

CONSONANTS

CONSONANTI

Most consonants are pronounced the same as in English, with the exception of the following:

- **c** - before **e** and **i**, it is pronounced like the **ch** in **ch**urch - *ci (chee)* - there
- **c** - before **o**, **a** and **u**, it is pronounced like the **k** in **k**ing - *casa (kah-zah)* - house
- **ch** - always pronounced like the **k** in **k**ing - *che (keh)* - that
- **g** - before **e** and **i**, it is pronounced like the **j** in **j**eep - *giro (jee-hroh)* - trip
- **g** - before **o**, **a** and **u**, it is pronounced like the **g** in **g**o - *gara (gah-rah)* - race, *guida (gwee-dah)* - guide
- **gh** - always pronounced like the **g** in **g**ate - *laghi (lah-ghee)* - lakes
- **gli** - pronounced like the **ll** in mi**ll**ion - *luglio (loo-l'yoh)* - July; *gli (l'yee)* - the

- **gn** - pronounced like the **ny** in ca**ny**on - *ogni (oh-n'yee)* - every
- **h** - not pronounced at all - *ha (ah)* - he has
- **qu** - pronounced like the **qu** in **qu**een - *qui (qwee)* - here
- **r** - rolled like the Scottish **r** - *caro (kah-roh)* - dear
- **s** - it is sharp (like the **s** in **s**ee) before other consonants: *strada (strah-dah)* - road; at the beginning of a word: *sala (sah-lah)* - hall; or when doubled: *sesso (sehs-soh)* - sex
- **s** - between two vowels, it is pronounced like the **z** in **z**ebra - *casa (kah-zah)* - home
- **sc** - before **i** and **e**, it is pronounced like the **sh** in **sh**eet - *sci (shee)* - ski
- **sc** - when followed by a consonant or by an **a**, **o** or **u**, it is pronounced like the **sk** in **sk**y - *scrivo (skree-voh)* - I write; *scusa (skoo-zah)* - sorry
- **z** - at the beginning of a word, it is pronounced like the **ds** in su**ds**y - *zero (dzeh-roh)* - zero
- **z** - elsewhere in a word, it is pronounced like the **ts** in gu**ts**y - *pranzo (prahn-tsoh)* - lunch

GENERAL

GENERALE

When speaking Italian, you should linger on the vowels and not pronounce the consonants too forcefully, except where a consonant has been doubled – e.g. *ditta (deet-tah)*.

Inflection is also important. Remember to make your voice rise at the end of a sentence if it is a question, and to modulate your voice downwards if it is a statement, just as you would when speaking English.

Practise a few phrases in Italian to get the hang of it – stressed syllables are underlined:

Ciao!
chaao
Hello!

Arrivederci!
arreevaydehrchee
Goodbye!

Parla inglese?
parla eengglaysay
Do you speak English?

Non capisco!
Non kapeesko
I don't understand!

Può parlare più lentamente, per favore?
pwo parlaaray peeoo layntamayntay, pehr favoray
Could you please speak more slowly?

Come sta?
komay sta
How are you? (polite)

Come stai?
komay stai
How are you? (familiar)

Bene, grazie!
Baynay graatseeay
Fine, thanks!

Scusi?
skoozee
Pardon?

Per favore!
pehr favoray
Please!

Grazie!
graatseeay
Thank you!

Posso avere ...?
posso avayray
May I have ...?

Vorrei ...
vorrehee
I'd like ...

Ieri
ee-ehree
yesterday

oggi
odjee
today

domani
domaanee
tomorrow

Dov'è la toilette?
doveh la toehlehteh
Where is the toilet?

NOUNS 15
NOMI 15

ADJECTIVES 16
AGGETTIVI 16

ARTICLES 17
ARTICOLI 17

VERBS 19
VERBI 19

The grammar section has deliberately been kept very brief as this is not a language course.

NOUNS

NOMI

All nouns are either masculine or feminine in **gender**. Masculine nouns usually end in **–o**, while feminine nouns usually end in **–a**. Nouns ending in **-e** can be either masculine or feminine, but their gender can be identified by referring to the definite article ('the') placed before the noun, e.g.

- *il ristorante* - masculine, as *il* is masculine
- *la chiave* - feminine, as *la* is feminine

Some nouns ending in **-a** refer to both men and women, e.g.

- *l'artista* (m/f) - the artist

To form the **plural** of a noun, all you need to do is change the last letter. Nouns ending in **-o** and **-e** will end in **-i** in their plural form, while those ending in **-a** will end in **-e** in their plural form. When changing a noun to the plural form, remember to make the definite article ('the') plural too (see page 18).

ADJECTIVES
AGGETTIVI

Adjectives must agree in **gender** and **number** with the noun they modify. In Italian, the adjective generally follows the noun, e.g.

- *un gatto bianco* – a white cat

Sometimes the adjective precedes the noun, for instance when expressing size, e.g.

- *una grande casa* – a large house

The **comparative** is formed by placing *piú* (more) or *meno* (less) before the adjective:

- large – *grande*; larger – *piú grande*
- ugly – *brutto*; less ugly – *meno brutto*

The **superlative** is formed either by placing *il/la/i/le piú* (the most) or *il/la/i/le meno* (the least) before the adjective, or by changing the ending of the adjective to -issimo (if used with a masculine noun) or -issima (if used with a feminine noun), e.g.

- very beautiful – *bellissimo, bellissima*

Possessive adjectives, like all adjectives, must agree in gender and number with the

noun they modify, with the exception of *loro* (their):

Masculine	Singular	Plural
my	*il mio*	*i miei*
your (fam)	*il tuo*	*i tuoi*
your (pol)	*il Suo*	*i Suoi*
his/hers/its	*il suo*	*i suoi*
our	*il nostro*	*i nostri*
your (pl)	*il vostro*	*i vostri*
their	*il loro*	*i loro*

Feminine	Singular	Plural
my	*la mia*	*le mie*
your (fam)	*la tua*	*le tue*
your (pol)	*la Sua*	*le Sue*
his/hers/its	*la sua*	*le sue*
our	*la nostra*	*le nostre*
your (pl)	*la vostra*	*le vostre*
their	*la loro*	*le loro*

ARTICLES

ARTICOLI

The **indefinite** article ('a' or 'an') is used as follows:

- ***un*** – before most masculine nouns

- ***uno*** - before masculine nouns beginning with **z** or **s** plus a consonant
- ***una*** - before most feminine nouns
- ***un'*** - before all feminine nouns beginning with a vowel

The **definite** article ('the') is used as follows:

- ***il*** - before most masculine singular nouns
- ***i*** - before most masculine plural nouns
- ***lo*** - before masculine singular nouns beginning with **z** or **s** plus a consonant
- ***gli*** - before masculine plural nouns beginning with **z** or **s** plus a consonant
- ***l'*** - before masculine singular nouns beginning with a vowel
- ***gli*** - before masculine plural nouns beginning with a vowel
- ***la*** - before most feminine singular nouns
- ***le*** - before most feminine plural nouns
- ***l'*** - before feminine singular nouns beginning with a vowel
- ***le*** - before feminine plural nouns beginning with a vowel

Since the article varies depending on the inflection (case), the gender of a noun in the

dictionary section is only stated as **m** (masculine) or **f** (feminine). A sustained effort is required to memorize all the genders and declensions, but this is not vital in order to make yourself understood.

VERBS

VERBI

There are three types of **regular** verbs in Italian, the infinitive forms of which end in **-are**, **-ere** or **-ire**. To form the **present** tense of these verbs, simply add different endings to the root, e.g. *portare* (to carry):

- port + **o** = *porto* – I carry
- port + **i** = *porti* – you (fam) carry
- port + **a** = *porta* – he/she carries
- port + **iamo** = *portiamo* – we carry
- port + **ate** = *portate* – you (pl) carry
- port + **ano** = *portano* – they carry

The present tense is formed in the same way for verbs ending in **-ere**, but the endings are slightly different: **-o**, **-i**, **-e**, **-iamo**, **-ete** and **-ono**. The endings for verbs ending in **-ire** are **-o**, **-i**, **-e**, **-iamo**, **-ite** and **-ono**.

The **future** tense for verbs ending in **-ere** and **-ire** is formed by removing the final **-e** and adding **-ò, -ai, -à, -emo, -ete** and **-anno**. For verbs ending **-are**, the **a** changes to **e** and the same endings are used, e.g. *portare* (to carry): *porter**ò**, porter**ai**, porter**à**, porter**emo**, porter**ete**, porter**anno***.

To make a verb **negative**, add *non* directly before the verb, e.g.

- *Capisco* – I understand
- *Non capisco* – I don't understand

Familiarize yourself with the present and past tense of some **auxiliary verbs** (for instance 'to be' and 'to have'), which are **irregular** verbs:

Present tense (to be – *essere*)

I am	*io sono*
you (fam) are	*tu sei*
you (pol) are	*Lei è*
he/she is	*lui/lei è*
we are	*noi siamo*
you (pl) are	*voi siete*
they are	*loro sono*

Past tense (to be - *essere*)

I was	*io ero*
you (fam) were	*tu eri*
you (pol) were	*Lei era*
he/she was	*lui/lei era*
we were	*noi eravamo*
you (pl) were	*voi eravate*
they were	*loro erano*

Present tense (to have - *avere*)

I have	io ho
you (fam) have	tu hai
you (pol) have	Lei ha
he/she has	lui/lei ha
we have	noi abbiamo
you (pl) have	voi avete
they have	loro hanno

Past tense (to have - *avere*)

I had	io avevo
you (fam) had	tu avevi
you (pol) had	Lei aveva
he/she had	lui/lei aveva
we had	noi avevamo
you (pl) had	voi avevate
they had	loro avevano

NUMBERS 23
NUMERI 23

DAYS 24
GIORNI 24

MONTHS 24
MESI 24

TIME 25
ORA 25

GREETINGS 26
SALUTI 26

GENERAL 27
GENERALE 27

FORMS AND SIGNS 28
MODULI E SEGNALI STRADALI 28

NUMBERS
NUMERI

0 zero *(tzai-ro)*
1 uno *(oo-no)*
2 due *(doo-ay)*
3 tre *(tray)*
4 quattro *(kwatt-ro)*
5 cinque *(cheen-kway)*
6 sei *(say)*
7 sette *(sett-ay)*
8 otto *(ott-o)*
9 nove *(noh-vay)*
10 dieci *(dee-ay-chee)*
11 undici *(oon-dee-chee)*
12 dodici *(doh-dee-chee)*
13 tredici *(tray-dee-chee)*
14 quattordici *(kwa-ttor-dee-chee)*
15 quindici *(kween-dee-chee)*
16 sedici *(say-dee-chee)*
17 diciassette *(dee-cha-se-ttay)*
18 diciotto *(dee-cho-tto)*
19 diciannove *(dee-chan-no-vay)*
20 venti *(ven-tee)*
21 ventuno *(ven-too-no)*
22 ventidue *(ven-tee-doo-ay)*
30 trenta *(tren-ta)*
31 trentuno *(tren-too-no)*
40 quaranta *(kwa-ran-ta)*
50 cinquanta *(cheen-kwan-ta)*
60 sessanta *(se-ssan-ta)*
70 settanta *(se-ttan-ta)*
80 ottanta *(o-ttan-ta)*
90 novanta *(no-van-ta)*
100 cento *(chen-to)*
101 centouno *(chen-too-no)*
120 centoventi *(chen-to-ven-tee)*
500 cinquecento *(cheen-kway-chen-to)*
1000 mille *(mee-lay)*
1 million un milione *(oon meel-yo-nay)*

DAYS
GIORNI

Monday
lunedì *(loo-ne-dee)*

Tuesday
martedì *(mar-te-dee)*

Wednesday
mercoledì
(mer-ko-le-dee)

Thursday
giovedì *(jo-ve-dee)*

Friday
venerdì *(ve-ner-dee)*

Saturday
sabato *(sa-ba-toh)*

Sunday
domenica *(do-me-nee-ka)*

weekdays
giorni feriali
(jor-nee fe-ree-aa-lee)

weekend
fine settimana
(fee-nay se-ttee-ma-na)

public holidays
giorni festivi
(jor-nee fes-tee-vee)

MONTHS
MESI

January
gennaio *(je-na-yo)*

February
febbraio *(feb-ra-yo)*

March
marzo *(mar-tso)*

April
aprile *(a-pree-le)*

May
maggio *(ma-jo)*

June
giugno *(joon-yo)*

July
luglio *(lool-yo)*

August
agosto *(a-gos-to)*

September
settembre *(se-tem-bre)*

October
ottobre *(o-to-bre)*

November
novembre *(no-vem-bre)*

December
dicembre *(dee-chem-bre)*

TIME
ORA

in the morning
di mattina
(dee ma-ttee-na)

in the afternoon
di pomeriggio
(dee po-me-ree-jo)

in the evening
di sera *(dee seh-ra)*

What is the time?
Che ora è?
(kay oh-ra eh)

- **it's three o'clock**
- sono le tre
  (soh-no le tre)

- **it's half past two**
- sono le due e mezza
  (soh-no le doo-ay eh met-sa)

- **it's quarter to three**
- sono le tre meno quindici *(soh-no le tre meh-no kween-dee-chee)*

- **twenty past two**
- sono le due e venti
  (soh-no le doo-ay eh ven-tee)

- **early**
- presto *(pres-toh)*

- **late**
- tardi *(tar-dee)*

at 10 a.m. (10:00)
alle dieci di mattina
(allay dee-ay-chee dee ma-ttee-na)

at 5 p.m. (17:00)
alle cinque di pomeriggio
(allay cheen-kway dee po-me-ree-jo)

today
oggi *(o-jee)*

tomorrow
domani *(do-ma-nee)*

yesterday
ieri *(yee-ree)*

day after tomorrow
dopodomani
(do-po-do-ma-nee)

day before yesterday
l'altro ieri *(lal-troh yee-ree)*

this morning
stamattina
(sta-ma-ttee-na)

yesterday evening
ieri sera *(yee-ree seh-ra)*

tomorrow morning
domani mattina
(do-ma-nee ma-ttee-na)

last night
ieri sera/notte
(yee-ree seh-ra/noh-ttay)

this week
questa settimana
(kwes-ta se-ttee-ma-na)

next week
la settimana prossima
(la se-ttee-ma-na pro-ssee-ma)

now
addesso *(a-deh-sso)*

What is today's date?
Che data è oggi?
(kay da-ta eh o-jee)

It's 20 December
È il venti dicembre *(eh eel ven-tee dee-chem-bre)*

GREETINGS
SALUTI

Good morning
Buongiorno
(bwon-jor-no)

Good evening
Buonasera
(bwo-na-say-ra)

Good night
Buonanotte
(bwo-na-no-ttay)

Hello/Cheerio
Ciao *(chaa-o)*

Goodbye
Arrivederci
(a-rree-vay-dehr-chee)

See you soon
A presto *(ah pres-toh)*

See you later
A più tardi
(ah pew tar-dee)

Have a good trip
Buon viaggio
(bwon vee-a-jo)

Take care!
Fa attenzione!
(fa a-tten-see-o-ne)

Have a good time
Divertitevi
(dee-ver-tee-te-vee)

I have to go now
Adesso devo andare
(a-deh-sso de-voh an-daa-re)

It was very nice
È stato un piacere
(eh staa-to oon pee-a-chay-ray)

My name is ...
Mi chiamo ...
(mee kee-a-mo ...)

What is your name?
Come ti chiami? (fam)
(ko-may tee kee-a-mee)
Come si chiama? (pol)
(ko-may see kee-a-ma)

Pleased to meet you!
Piacere! *(pee-a-chay-ray)*

How are you?
Come sta? (pol.)
(ko-may stah)
Come stai? (fam.)
(ko-may staa-y)

Just a minute
Un minuto solo
(oon mee-noo-to so-lo)

GENERAL
GENERALE

Do you speak English?
Parla inglese?
(paar-la een-glay-say)

I don't understand
Non capisco
(non ka-pees-ko)

Please speak very slowly
Può parlare più lentamente, per favore
(pwo paar-laar-ay pew len-ta-mehn-tay, pehr fa-vo-ray)

Please repeat that
Può ripetere, per favore
(pwo ree-pe-te-ray, pehr fa-vo-ray)

Please write it down
Lo scriva, per favore *(loh skree-va, pehr fa-vo-ray)*

Excuse me please
Mi scusi, per favore *(mee skoo-see, pehr fa-vo-re)*

Could you help me?
Mi può aiutare.
(mee pwo a-yoo-ta-ray)

Could you do me a favour?
Mi può fare un favore?
(mee pwo faa-re oon fa-vo-ray

Can you show me ...
Può indicarmi ...
(pwo een-dee-char-mee)

how?
come? *(ko-may)*

where?
dove? *(do-veh)*

when?
quando? *(kwan-do)*

who?
chi? *(kee)*

why?
perchè? *(payr-keh)*

which?
quale? *(kwaa-leh)*

I need ...
Ho bisogno ...
(O bee-son-yo)

thank you
grazie *(graat-see-ay)*

yes/no
sì/no *(see/noh)*

FORMS & SIGNS
MODULI E SEGNALI STRADALI

Please complete in block letters
Completare in lettere maiuscole, per favore
(kom-ple-taa-ray in le-tte-ray ma-yoo-sko-lay, pehr fa-vo-ray)

Surname
Cognome *(kog-no-may)*

First name
Nome di battesimo *(no-may dee ba-ttay-see-mo)*

Date of birth
Data di nascita *(dah-ta dee na-shee-ta)*

Place of birth
Luogo di nascita
(lwo-go dee na-shee-ta)

Occupation
Mestiere *(mes-tee-ay-ray)*

Nationality
Nazionalità
(nat-see-o-na-lee-ta)

Address
Indirizzo
(een-dee-ree-tso)

Passport Number
Numero di passaporto
(noo-me-ro dee pa-ssa-pohr-to)

I.D. Number
Numero d'identità *(noo-me-ro dee-den-tee-ta)*

Issued at
Rilasciato a
(ree-la-shee-at-o ah)

Date of arrival
Data di arrivo
(da-ta dee a-rree-vo)

Date of departure
Data di partenza
(da-ta dee par-tehn-tsa)

Engaged, Vacant
Occupato, Libero
(ok-koo-pa-to, lee-be-ro)

No trespassing
I trasgressori saranno puniti
(ee tras-gray-sso-ree sah-ran-no poo-neetee)

Out of order
Guasto *(gwoo-as-to)*

Don't disturb
Non disturbare
(non dees-toor-ba-ray)

Push, Pull
Spingere, Tirare
(speen-ge-ray, tee-ra-ray)

Adults and Children
Adulti e Bambini *(a-dool-tee eh bam-bee-nee)*

Lift/Elevator
Ascensore *(a-shen-so-ray)*

Escalator
Scala mobile
(skaa-la mo-bee-lay)

Wet paint
Vernice fresca
(ver-nee-che fres-ka)

Open, Closed
Aperto, Chiuso
(a-pehr-to, kee-oo-so)

Till/Cash Desk
Cassa *(kas-sa)*

Opening hours
Orario di apertura *(o-ra-ree-o dee a-per-too-ra)*

Self-service
Servirsi da soli
(ser-veer-see da so-lee)

Waiting Room
Sala d'aspetto
(saa-la das-peh-tto)

BUS/TRAM STOP 31
FERMATA DELL'AUTOBUS/
FERMATA DEL TRAM 31

UNDERGROUND/SUBWAY/METRO 31
LA METROPOLITANA 31

TRAIN/RAILWAY 32
IL TRENO/LA FERROVIA 32

BOATS 34
NAVI 34

TAXI 35
TASSÌ/TAXI 35

AIRPORT 35
AEROPORTO 35

ROAD TRAVEL/CAR HIRE 37
VIAGGIARE PER STRADA/
NOLEGGIO AUTOMOBILI 37

SIGNS 38
SEGNALI STRADALI 38

BUS/TRAM STOP
FERMATA DELL'AUTO-BUS/FERMATA DEL TRAM

Where is the bus/tram stop?
Dov'è la fermata dell'autobus/del tram?
(do-veh la fayr-maa-ta dell ow-to-boos/dell tram)

Which bus do I take?
Quale autobus devo prendere? *(kwa-lay ow-to-boos day-vo prayn-day-ray)*

How often do the buses go?
Ogni quanto passa l'autobus? *(on-yee kwan-to pah-ssah l'ow-to-boos)*

When is the last bus?
Quando è l'ultimo autobus? *(kwan-do eh lool-tee-mo ow-to-boos)*

Punch your ticket
Validate il biglietto *(va-lee-daa-tay il beel-yay-tto)*

I want to go to ...
Voglio andare a ...
(vol-yo an-daa-ray ah ...)

What is the fare to ...?
Quant'è il biglietto per ...?
(kwan-teh il beel-yay-tto pehr ...)

Which ticket must I buy?
Quale biglietto devo comperare?
(kwa-lay beel-yay-tto day-vo kom-pe-raa-ray)

When is the next bus?
Quando è il prossimo autobus?
(kwan-do eh il pro-ssee-mo ow-to-boos)

UNDERGROUND/ SUBWAY/METRO
LA METROPOLITANA

entrance, exit
entrata, uscita *(en-traa-tah, oo-shee-tah)*

Where is the underground station?
Dov'è la stazione della metropolitana?
(do-veh la stat-sy-o-ne day-lla may-tro-po-lee-taa-na)

inner zone, outer zone
Zona interna, zona esterna *(tso-nah in-tehr-na, tso-nah es-tehr-na)*

Do you have a map for the metro?
Avete una carta della metropolitana? *(a-veh-teh oo-na kar-ta day-lla may-tro-po-lee-taa-na)*

I want to go to ...
Voglio andare a ...
(vol-yo an-daa-ray ah ...)

Can you give me change?
Puo' darmi il resto?
(pwo daar-mee il re-stoh)

Where must I go?
Dove devo andare? *(do-veh day-vo an-daa-ray)*

When is the next train?
Quando è il prossimo treno? *(kwan-do eh il pro-ssee-mo tray-no)*

How long will it be delayed?
Quanto c'è di ritardo?
(kwan-to cheh dee ree-taar-do)

TRAIN/RAILWAY
IL TRENO/ LA FERROVIA

Where is the railway station?
Dov'è la stazione ferroviaria? *(do-veh la sta-tsy-o-ne fe-rro-vee-a-ree-ah)*

departure
partenza *(paar-ten-sa)*

arrival
arrivo *(ar-ree-vo)*

Which platform?
Quale binario? *(kwaa-le bee-naa-ree-o)*

a ... ticket please
Un biglietto ... per favore
(oon beel-yay-tto ... pehr fa-vo-ray)

- **single**
- di sola andata
  (dee soh-lah an-daa-ta)

- **return**
- di andata e ritorno *(dee an-daa-ta eh ree-tor-no)*

- **child's**
- per minorenni
  (pehr mee-no-renn-ee)

- **first class**
- di prima classe (dee pree-ma klass-ay)

- **second class**
- di seconda classe (dee say-kon-da klass-ay)

- **smoking**
- per fumatori (pehr foo-ma-to-ree)

- **non-smoking**
- per non fumatori (pehr non foo-ma-to-ree)

Do I have to pay a supplement?
Devo pagare un supplemento? *(day-vo pa-gaa-ray oon soo-pleh-men-toh)*

Is my ticket valid on this train?
Il mio biglietto è valido su questo treno? *(il mee-o beel-yay-tto eh va-lee-do soo kwes-to tray-no)*

Where do I have to get off?
Dove devo scendere? *(do-veh day-vo shayn-day-ray)*

Do you have a timetable?
Avete un orario? *(a-veh-teh oo-na o-ra-ree-o)*

I want to book ...
Voglio prenotare ... *(vol-yo pre-no-taa-re ...)*

- **a seat**
- un posto (oon pos-to)

- **a couchette**
- una cuccetta (oo-na koo-chay-ttay)

Is this seat free?
È libero questo posto? *(eh lee-bay-ray kway-sto pos-to)*

That is my seat
Quello è il mio posto *(kwe-llo eh il mee-o pos-to)*

May I open (close) the window?
Posso aprire (chiudere) la finestra? *(pos-so a-pree-ray (kee-oo-de-ray) la fee-nay-stra)*

Where is the restaurant car?
Dov'è la carrozza ristorante? *(do-veh la kaa-rrot-sah rees-to-raan-tay)*

Is there a sleeper?
C'è un vagone letto?
(*Cheh oon va-go-nay leh-ttoh)*

EC - Eurocity
International express, supplement payable

IC - Intercity
Luxury international express, supplement payable

station master
capostazione
(ka-po-sta-tsy-o-ne)

BOATS
NAVI

cruise
crociera *(kro-chee-rah)*

Can we hire a boat?
Possiamo noleggiare una barca? *(po-ssee-a-mo no-lay-djaa-ray oo-na baar-ka)*

How much is a round trip?
Quanto costa un biglietto di andata e ritorno? *(kwan-to kos-ta oon beel-yay-tto dee an-daa-ta eh ree-tor-no)*

one ticket
un biglietto
(oon beel-yay-tto)

two tickets
due biglietti
(doo-ay beel-yay-ttee)

How long is the trip?
Quanto dura il viaggio?
(kwan-to doo-ra il vee-a-jee-o)

Can we eat on board?
Possiamo mangiare a bordo? *(po-ssee-a-mo man-jaa-re ah bohr-do)*

When is the last boat?
Quando è l'ultimo battello? *(kwan-do eh lool-timo ba-tteh-lloh)*

When is the next ferry?
Quando è il prossimo traghetto? *(kwan-do eh il pro-ssee-mo tra-gay-tto)*

Is the sea rough?
Il mare è mosso?
(il maa-re eh moh-sso)

I feel seasick
Ho mal di mare
(o mal dee maa-re)

TAXI
TASSÌ/TAXI

Please order me a taxi
Mi chiami un tassì, per favore *(mee kee-a-mee oon ta-ssee, pehr fa-vo-ray)*

Where can I get a taxi?
Dove si trovano un tassì?
(do-vay see tro-va-no oon ta-ssee)

To this address, please
A questo indirizzo, per favore *(ah kwes-to een-dee-ree-tzo, pehr fa-vo-ray)*

How much is it to the centre?
Quanto costa per andare in centro?
(kwan-to kos-ta pehr aan-daa-re in chen-tro)

To the airport, please
All'aeroporto, per favore
(*all-aay-ro-por-to, pehr fa-vo-ray)*

To the station, please
Alla stazione, per favore
(al-la sta-tsee-o-nay, pehr fa-vo-ray)

Keep the change
Tenga il resto
(ten-gha eel res-toh)

I need a receipt
Ho bisogno di una ricevuta
(*o bee-son-ya dee oo-na ree-ce-voo-ta)*

AIRPORT
AEROPORTO

arrival
arrivo *(a-rree-vo)*

departure
partenza *(paar-ten-sa)*

flight number
numero del volo
(noo-me-ro del vo-lo)

delay
ritardo *(ree-tardo)*

check-in
accettazione bagagli
(a-chay-tat-see-o-nay ba-gaa-lyee)

hand luggage
bagaglio a mano *(ba-gaa-lyee-o ah ma-no)*

boarding card
la carta d'imbarco
(la kar-ta deem-bar-ko)

gate
l'uscita *(loo-shee-ta)*

valid, invalid
valido, non valido *(va-lee-do, non va-lee-do)*

baggage/luggage claim
ritiro bagagli
(ree-tee-ro ba-gaa-lyee)

lost property office
l'ufficio oggetti smarriti
(loo-ffee-cho oh-jet-tee sma-rree-tee)

Where do I get a bus to the centre?
Dov'è l'autobus per il centro città? *(do-veh low-to-boos pehr il chen-tro chee-tta)*

Where do I check in for ...?
Dov'è il banco accettazione per ...? *(do-veh eel ban-ko a-chay-tat-see-o-nay pehr ...)*

An aisle/window seat, please
un posto sul corridoio/al finestrino per favore
(oon pos-to sool ko-rree-do-yo/al fee-nes-tree-no, pehr fa-vo-ray)

Where is the gate for the flight to ...?
Dov'è l'uscita per il volo a ...? *(do-veh loo-shee-ta pehr eel vo-lo ah ...)*

I have nothing to declare
Non ho niente da dichiarare *(non o nyen-tay da dee-kya-ra-ray)*

It's for my own personal use
È per il mio uso personale *(eh pehr eel mee-o oo-so per-so-naa-leh)*

The flight has been cancelled
Il volo è stato cancellato *(eel vo-lo eh staa-to kan-che-llaa-to)*

The flight has been delayed
Il volo è in ritardo *(eel vo-lo eh in ree-tar-do)*

ROAD TRAVEL/ CAR HIRE
VIAGGIARE PER STRADA/NOLEGGIO AUTOMOBILI

Have you got a road map?
Avete una carta stradale? *(a-veh-teh oo-na kar-ta stra-daa-le)*

How many kilometres is it to ...?
Quanti chilometri è lontano ...? *(kwan-tee kee-lo-may-tree eh lon-taa-no ...)*

Where is the nearest garage?
Dov'è l'autorimessa più vicina? *(do-veh low-to-ree-may-ssa pee-oo vee-chee-na)*

Fill it up, please
il pieno, per favore *(eel pee-ay-no, pehr fa-vo-ray)*

Please check the oil, water, battery, tyres
Per favore, controlli l'olio, l'acqua, la batteria, le gomme *(pehr fa-vo-ray, kon-tro-llee lo-lee-o, lak-wa, la ba-tte-ree-a, le gom-meh)*

I'd like to hire a car
Vorrei noleggiare un'automobile *(vo-re-hee no-lay-djaa-ray oon-ow-to-mo-bee-le)*

How much does it cost per week/day?
Quanto costa alla settimana/al giorno? *(kwan-to kos-ta al-la say-ttee-maa-na/al jor-no)*

What do you charge per kilometre?
Quanto costa al chilometro? *(kwan-to kos-ta al kee-lo-may-tro)*

Is the mileage unlimited?
il chilometraggio è senza limite? *(eel kee-lo-may-tra-jo eh sen-sa lee-mee-te)*

Where can I pick up the car?
Dove ritiro l'automobile? *(do-veh ree-tee-ro low-to-mo-bee-le)*

Where can I leave the car?
Dove lascio l'automobile? *(do-veh la-shee-o ow-to-mo-bee-le)*

garage
autorimessa, garage *(ow-to-ree-may-ssa, garage)*

headlight
fari dell'automobile *(faa-ree del-low-to-mo-bee-le)*

windscreen
parabrezza *(pa-ra-bret-sa)*

windscreen wiper
tergicristallo *(ter-gee-krees-tal-lo)*

What is the speed limit?
Quanto è il limite della velocita? *(kwan-to eh ee lee-mee-te day-la ve-lo-chee-ta)*

The keys are locked in the car
Le chiavi sono chiuse nella macchina *(le kee-aa-vee so-no kee-oo-se nel-la ma-kkee-na)*

The engine is overheating
Il motore è troppo caldo *(eel mo-to-reh eh trop-poh kal-do)*

Have you got ...
Avete ...? *(a-veh-teh ...)*

◆ **a towing rope**
◆ un cavo per rimorchiare *(oon ka-vo pehr ree-mor-kee-a-ray)*

◆ **a screwdriver/ spanner**
◆ un cacciavite/una chiave inglese *(oon ka-chee-a-vee-te/oo-na kee-aa-vee een-glay-say)*

SIGNS
SEGNALI STRADALI

No through road
Divieto di transito *(dee-veeh-to dee tran-see-to)*

one-way street
senso unico *(sen-so oo-ni-ko)*

entrance
entrata *(en-traa-tah)*

exit
uscita *(oo-shee-tah)*

Keep entrance clear
Passo carrabile *(pa-sso ka-rra-bee-le)*

Residents only
Solo residenti *(so-lo re-see-den-tee)*

pedestrians
pedoni *(pe-do-nee)*

danger
pericolo *(pe- ree-co-lo)*

speed limit
Il limite di velocità *(eel lee-mee-te dee ve-lo-chee-ta)*

No entry
Divieto di accesso *(dee-vee-hto dee a-che-sso)*

roundabout
Rotonda *(roh-ton-da)*

Toll
Pedaggio *(pe-da-jee-o)*

Insert coins
Inserire monete *(een-se-ree-ray mo-ne-teh)*

Returned coins
Monete di resto
(mo-ne-teh dee res-toh)

No parking
Sosta vietata
(sos-tah vee-ay-ta-ta)

paying car park
parcheggio a pagamento
(par-kay-djo ah pa-ja-men-toh

unattended car park
parcheggio incustidito
(par-kay-djo in-coo-sto-dee-to)

No right turn
Svolta a destra proibita
(svol-ta ah day-stra pro-ee-bee-ta)

cul de sac
vicolo cieco
(vee-ko-lo chee-ay-ko)

detour
deviazione *(de-vee-at-see-o-ne)*

No admission for un-authorized persons
Vietato l'accesso ai non autorizzati *(vee-ay-ta-to la-chess-o ay non ow-to-ree-tsaa-tee)*

Caution
Attenzione
(a-tten-see-o-nay)

No stopping
Sosta vietata
(sos-tah vee-ay-ta-ta)

No overtaking
Vietato il sorpasso
(vee-ay-ta-to eel sor-paa-ssoh)

ACCOMMODATION 41
ALLOGGIO 41

RECEPTION 43
RICEVIMENTO 43

SELF-CATERING 44
ALLOGGIO SELF-SERVICE 44

CAMPING 46
CAMPEGGIO 46

ACCOMMODATION
ALLOGGIO

hotel
albergo *(al-bayr-go)*

bed & breakfast
camera e prima colazione *(ka-may-ra eh pree-ma ko-la-tsyo-ne)*

vacancies
camere libere *(ka-may-reh lee-be-ray)*

Have you a room ...?
Avete una camera ...?
(a-ve-teh oo-na ka-may-ra ...)

- **for tonight**
- per stanotte
  (pehr sta-noh-tte)

- **with breakfast**
- con prima colazione
  (kon pree-ma ko-la-tsy-o-ne)

- **with bath**
- con bagno
  (kon ban-yo)

- **with shower**
- con doccia
  (kon dot-cha)

- **single room**
- camera singola
  (ka-may-ra seen-go-la)

- **double room**
- camera doppia
  (ka-may-ra do-ppee-a)

- **family room**
- camera per famiglia
  (ka-may-ra pehr fa-mee-lya)

How much is the room ...?
Quanto costa la camera ...? *(kwan-to kos-ta la ka-may-ra)*

- **per day/week**
- al giorno/alla settimana
  (al jor-no/al-la set-tee-maa-na)

Have you got anything cheaper/ better?
Ne avete un'altra che costa meno/migliore?
(neh a-ve-teh oon-al-trah kay kos-ta me-noh/mee-lee-o-reh)

May I see the room?
Posso vedere la camera?
(pos-so ve-de-ray la ka-may-ra)

Do you have a cot?
Avete un lettino? *(a-ve-teh oon le-ttee-noh)*

What time is breakfast/dinner?
A che ora è la prima colazione/il pranzo? *(a kay o-rah eh la pree-ma ko-la-tsy-o-ne/eel prant-so)*

room service
servizio in camera *(sayr-vee-tsee-o in ka-may-ra)*

Please bring ...
Per favore portatemi ... *(pehr fa-vo-ray por-ta-te-mee)*

- **toilet paper**
- la carta igienica *(la kar-ta ee-jee-nee-ka)*

- **clean towels**
- degli asciugamani puliti *(day-lee a-shoo-ga-maa-nee poo-lee-tee*

Please clean ...
Per favore pulite ... *(pehr fa-vo-ray poo-lee-te)*

- **the bath/washbasin**
- il bagno/lavandino *(eel baan-yo/la-van-dee-no)*

Please put fresh sheets on the bed
Per favore cambiate le lenzuola *(pehr fa-vo-ray kam-bee-at-ay leh len-tswo-la)*

Please don't touch ...
Vi prego di non toccare ... *(vee pre-goh dee non to-kaa-reh)*

- **my briefcase**
- la mia borsa *(la mee-a bor-sah)*

- **my laptop**
- il mio laptop *(eel mee-o laptop)*

My ... doesn't work
La ... non funziona *(la... non foon-see-o-na*

- **toilet**
- toilette *(toy-let-te)*

- **bedside lamp**
- lampada da letto *(lam-pa-dah da leh-tto)*

There is no hot water
Non c'è aqua calda *(non che ak-wa kal-da)*

RECEPTION
RICEVIMENTO

Are there any messages for me?
Ci sono dei messaggi per me? *(chee so-no day me-ssa-jee)*

Has anyone asked for me?
Mi ha cercato qualcuno? *(mee a cher-ka-to kwal-koo-no)*

Can I leave a message for someone?
Posso lasciare un messaggio per qualcuno? *(pos-so la-shee-a-ray oon mess-a-jee-o pehr kwal-koo-no)*

Is there a laundry service?
Avete un servizio lavanderia? *(a-ve-teh oon ser-veet-see-o la-van-de-ree-a)*

I need a wake-up call at 7 o'clock
Debbo essere svegliato alle sette *(deb-boh e-sseh-reh sve-llee-a-to all-eh seh-tteh)*

What number must I dial for room service?
Che numero debbo fare per servizio in camera? *(kay noo-me-ro deb-boh faa-ray pehr ser-veet-see-o in ka-may-ra)*

Where is the lift/ elevator?
Dov'è l'ascensore? *(do-veh la-shayn-so-ray)*

Do you arrange tours?
Organizzate gite turistiche? *(or-ga-nee-zaa-tay jee-teh too-ree-stee-ke)*

Please prepare the bill
Preparate il conto per favore *(pre-pa-raa-tay eel kon-to pehr fa-vo-ray)*

There is a mistake in the bill
C'è un errore nel conto *(che oon ay-rro-ray nel kon-to)*

I'm leaving tomorrow
Parto domani *(paar-to do-ma-nee)*

SELF-CATERING
ALLOGGIO SELF-SERVICE

Have you any vacancies?
Avete camere libere?
(a-ve-teh ka-may-ra lee-be-ray)

How much is it per night/week?
Quanto costa alla notte/settimana? *(kwan-to kos-ta al-lah noh-tte/se-ttee-maa-na)*

How big is it?
Com'è grande?
(ko-may graan-day)

Do you allow children?
È permesso alloggiare bambini? *(eh pehr-mess-o allo-jee-a-ray bam-bee-nee)*

Please, show me how ... works
Per favore mi faccia vedere come funziona ...
(pehr fa-vo-ray mee fa-cha ve-de-ray ko-may foon-see-o-na)

- **the cooker/stove, the oven**
- la stufa, il forno *(la stoo-fa, eel for-noh)*

- **the washing machine**
- la lavatrice *(la la-va-tree-che)*

- **the dryer**
- l'asciugatrice *(la-shee-oo-ga-tree-che)*

- **the hair-dryer**
- l'asciugacapelli *(la-shee-oo-ga-ka-pel-lee)*

- **the heater**
- il riscaldamento *(eel rees-kal-da-men-toh)*

- **the water heater**
- il bollitore per l'acqua *(eel bo-llee-to-reh pehr lak-wa)*

Where is/are ...?
Dov'è/dove sono ...?
(do-veh so-no)

- **the switch**
- l'interruttore *(leen-te-rroo-tto-re)*

- **the fuses**
- I fusibili *(ee foo-see-bee-lee)*

Is there ...?
C'è ...? *(che)*

◆ **a cot**
◆ un lettino *(oon let-tee-no)*

◆ **a high chair**
◆ un seggiolone
(oon se-jee-o-lo-neh)

◆ **a safe**
◆ una cassaforte
(oo-na kas-sa-for-teh)

We need more ...
Ci servono più ...
(chee ser-von-oh pew ...)

◆ **cutlery**
◆ coltelleria *(kol-telle-ree-a)*

◆ **crockery**
◆ stoviglie *(sto-veel-yay)*

◆ **sheets**
◆ lenzuola *(lent-swo-la)*

◆ **blankets**
◆ coperte *(ko-per-teh)*

◆ **pillows**
◆ cuscini *(koo-shee-nee)*

Is there ... in the vicinity?
C'è ... qui vicino? *(che ... kwee vee-cee-no)*

◆ **a shop**
◆ un negozio
(oon ne-gots-yo)

◆ **a restaurant**
◆ un ristorante
(oon rees-to-ran-te)

◆ **a bus/tram**
◆ un autobus/un tram
(oon ow-to-boos/oon tram)

We would like to stay for ...
Vorremmo stare ...
(vor-rehm-mo sta-ray ...)

◆ **three nights**
◆ tre notti *(tre not-tee)*

◆ **one week**
◆ una settimana
(oo-na se-tee-maa-na)

I have locked myself out
Mi sono chiuso fuori *(mee so-no kee-oo-so fwo-ree)*

The window won't open/close
La finestra non si apre/chiude
(la fee-nes-trah non see a-pray/kee-oo-deh)

CAMPING
CAMPEGGIO

caravan
carovana *(ka-ro-va-na)*

Have you got a list of camp sites?
Avete una lista dei campeggi? *(a-ve-teh oo-na lees-ta day kam-pe-jee)*

Are there any sites available?
Ci sono dei posti liberi? *(chee so-no day pos-tee lee-be-ree)*

How much is it per night/week?
Quanto costa alla notte/ settimana? *(kwan-to kos-ta al-la noh-tte/ set-tee-maa-na)*

Can we park the caravan here?
Possiamo parcheggiare qui? *(pos-see-a-mo par-ke-jaa-ray kwee)*

Can we camp here overnight?
Possiamo pernottare qui? *(pos-see-a-mo per-noh-tta-ray kwee)*

This site is very muddy
Questo posto è pieno di fango *(kwes-to poh-sto eh pee-ay-no dee fan-goh)*

Is there a sheltered site?
Non c'è un posto più riparato?
(non che oon poh-sto pew ree-pa-ra-toh)

Do you have electricity?
Avete l'elettricità? *(a-ve-teh le-lett-ree-chee-ta)*

Is there ... in the vicinity
C'è nei dintorni ...?
(che nay deen-tor-nee)

- **a shop**
- un negozio
  (oon ne-gots-yo

- **un restaurant**
- un ristorante
  (oon rees-to-ran-te)

- **an eating place**
- uno spaccio alimentari
  (oo-no spa-cho a-lee-men-ta-ree)

◆ **a garage**
◆ un autorimessa *(oon ow-to-ree-mes-sa)*

We would like to stay for ...
Vorremmo stare ... *(vo-rreh-mmo staa-ray)*

◆ **three nights**
◆ tre notti *(tre not-tee)*

◆ **one week**
◆ una settimana *(oo-na se-ttee-maa-na)*

Is there drinking water?
C'è acqua potabile? *(che ak-wa po-ta-bee-leh)*

Can I light a fire here?
Posso fare un fuoco qui? *(pos-so faa-ray oon fwo-ko kwee)*

I'd like to buy fire wood
Vorrei comprare della legna *(vor-ray kom-pra-ray del-la len-ya)*

Is the wood dry?
La legna è asciutta? *(la len-ya eh a-shee-oo-tta)*

Do you have ... for rent?
Avete ... da affittare? *(a-ve-teh ... da a-ffee-ta-ray)*

◆ **a tent**
◆ una tenda *(oo-na ten-da)*

◆ **a gas cylinder**
◆ una bombola di gas *(oo-na bom-bo-lah dee gas)*

◆ **a groundsheet**
◆ un telone impermeabile *(oon te-lo-neh eem-per-me-a-bee-lay)*

◆ **cooking utensils**
◆ degli utensili di cucina *(day-lee oo-ten-see-lee dee ku-chee-na)*

Where is the nearest ...?
Dov'è i/la/il ... più vicino? *(do-veh ee/la/eel ...pew vee-cee-no)*

◆ **toilet block**
◆ gabinetti *(ga-bee-net-tee)*

◆ **sink (for washing dishes)**
◆ secchiaio *(se-kee-ay-o)*

CUTLERY 49
POSATE 49

BREAKFAST 49
PRIMA COLAZIONE 49

LUNCH/DINNER 50
IL PRANZO/LA CENA 50

DRINKS 51
BEVANDE 51

FOOD 53
CIBO 53

DESSERTS & CAKES 57
DOLCI & TORTE 57

CUTLERY
POSATE

knife
coltello *(kol-tell-oh)*

fork, cake fork
forchetta, forchetta da torta *(for-ke-ttah, for-ke-ttah dah tor-tah)*

spoon, teaspoon
cucchiaio, cucchiaino *(koo-kya-yo, koo-kya-ee-no)*

crockery
stoviglie *(sto-veel-yay)*

plate
piatto *(pee-att-oh)*

cup and saucer, mug
tazza e piattino. boccale *(tat-sah eh pee-a-tee-noh, bo-kaa-leh)*

BREAKFAST
PRIMA COLAZIONE

coffee
caffè *(kaf-fay)*

◆ **black**
◆ nero *(nai-roh)*

◆ **with milk, cream**
◆ con latte, panna per il caffè *(kon lat-tay, pah-nnah pehr eel kaf-fay)*

◆ **without sugar**
◆ senza zucchero *(sen-tsa tzoo-kai-roh)*

tea
tè *(tay)*

◆ **with milk, lemon**
◆ con latte, limone *(kon lat-tay, lee-mo-nay)*

bread
pane *(paa-nay)*

rolls
panini *(paa-nee-nee)*

egg(s) ...
uovo/uova ... *(wo-vo/wo-va ...)*

◆ **boiled – soft, hard**
◆ bollito – alla coque, sodo *(bo-lee-to – al-lah kok-way, soh-doh)*

◆ **fried**
◆ fritte *(free-ttay)*

◆ **scrambled**
◆ strapazzate *(stra-patt-saa-tay)*

◆ **poached**
◆ in camicia
(in ka-mee-cha)

bacon and eggs
pancetta e uova
(pan-chet-ta eh wo-va)

cereal
cereali *(che-re-al-ee)*

hot milk, cold milk
latte caldo, latte freddo
(lat-tay kal-do, lat-tay fred-doh)

fruit
frutta *(froo-tta)*

orange juice
succo d'arancia
(zoo-koh da-ran-chay)

jam
marmellata
(mar-may-llaa-ta)

marmalade
marmellata d'arance
(mar-may-llaa-ta da-ran-chay)

pepper
pepe *(peh-peh)*

salt
sale *(saa-leh)*

LUNCH/DINNER
IL PRANZO/LA CENA

Could we have a table ...?
Possiamo avere una tavola ...? *(pos-see-aa-mo a-vay-ray oo-na ta-voh-lah ...)*

◆ **outside**
◆ fuori *(fwo-ree)*

◆ **inside**
◆ dentro *(den-troh)*

May I have ... ?
Posso avere ... ?
(pos-so a-vay-ray ...)

◆ **the menu**
◆ il menù *(eel me-noo)*

◆ **the wine list**
◆ la lista dei vini
(la lees-ta day vee-nee)

◆ **the menu of the day**
◆ il menù del giorno *(eel me-noo del jor-no)*

◆ **the snack list**
◆ la lista degli spuntini
(la lees-ta day-lee spoon-tee-nee)

◆ **starters**
◆ gli antipasti
(lyee an-tee-pas-tee)

◆ **main course**
◆ la portata principale
(la por-taa-ta preen-chee-paa-le)

◆ **dessert**
◆ il dolce *(eel dol-chay)*

I'll take the set menu
Scelgo il menù fisso
(skayl-goh eel me-noo fee-sso)

What is this?
Che cos' è questo?
(kay ko-zay eh kwes-to)

That is not what I ordered
Non ho ordinato questo
(non o or-dee-naa-to kwes-to)

It's tough, cold, off
È duro, freddo, avariato
(eh doo-ro, freh-ddo, a-va-ree-a-to)

What do you recommend?
Che cosa raccomanda?
(kay ko-za ra-ko-maan-da)

Can I have the bill please?
Il conto per favore? *(eel kon-to pehr fa-vo-ray)*

We'd like to pay separately
Vorremmo pagare separatamente *(vo-rreh-mmo pa-gaa-ray say-pa-ra-ta-mayn-tay)*

There is a mistake
C'è un errore
(che oon eh-rro-ray)

Thank you, that's for you
Grazie, questo è per voi
(graat-see-ay, kwes-to eh pehr voy)

Keep the change
Tenga il resto
(tayn-ga eel reh-sto)

DRINKS
BEVANDE

a beer/lager large, small
una birra
grande, piccola
(oo-na beer-ra gran-day, pee-ko-la)

half a liter
mezzo litro
(met-so lee-tro)

amaro (bitter liqueur)
amaro *(a-maa-roh)*

grappa (grape spirits)
grappa *(grah-pa)*

maraschino
maraschino
(ma-ras-kee-no)

a dry white wine
un vino bianco secco
(oon vee-no bee-an-ko sek-ko)

a sweet white wine
un vino bianco dolce
(oon vee-no bee-an-ko dol-chay)

a light red wine
un vino rosso leggero
(oon vee-no roh-sso lay-je-roh)

a full-bodied red wine
un vino rosso robusto
(oon vee-no roh-sso ro-boos-to)

a bottle
una bottiglia
(oo-na bo-tteel-ya)

a glass
un bicchiere *(oon beek-yai-ray)*

sparkling wine
spumante
(spoo-man-tay)

house wine
vino di casa
(vee-no dee ka-za)

brandy
cognac *(kon-yak)*

whisky with ice
whisky con ghiaccio
(whisky kon gee-a-cho)

whisky without ice
whisky senza ghiaccio
(whisky sen-sa gee-a-cho)

mineral water – still, sparkling
acqua minerale – naturale, frizzante *(ak-wa mee-nay-raa-lay – na-too-raa-lay, freet-san-tay)*

tap water
acqua normale
(ak-wa nor-maa-lay)

fruit juice
succo di frutta
(zoo-koh dee froo-tta)

tomato juice
succo di pomodoro *(zoo-koh dee po-moh-doh-roh)*

liqueur
liquore *(lee-kwo-ray)*

another ... please
un'altro ... per favore *(oon-al-troh ... pehr fa-vo-ray)*

too cold
troppo freddo *(trop-po freh-ddo)*

not cold enough
non è freddo abbastanza *(non eh freh-ddo abba-stant-sa)*

FOOD
CIBO

SOUP
MINESTRA *(mee-nes-tra)*

potato soup, mush-room soup
minestra di patate, funghi *(mee-nes-tra dee pa-ta-tay, foon-gee)*

celery and rice soup
minestra di sedano e riso *(mee-nes-tra dee say-da-no eh ree-so)*

pea, bean, lentil soup
minestra di piselli, fagioli, lenticchie *(mee-nes-tra dee pee-sell-ee, fa-jo-lee, len-teek-yay)*

noodle soup
minestra con pastina *(mee-nes-tra kon pas-tee-na)*

thick vegetable soup with noodles
minestrone *(mee-nes-tro-nay)*

FISH
PESCE *(pe-shay)*

sole
sogliola *(sol-yo-la)*

mackerel
sgombro *(sghom-broh)*

cuttlefish
seppia *(sep-pee-a)*

cod
merluzzo *(mair-loo-tzo)*

salmon
salmone *(sal-mo-nay)*

herring
arringa *(a-reen-ga)*

trout
trota *(troh-ta)*

turbot
rombo *(rohm-bo)*

tuna
tonno *(tohn-no)*

fried, grilled, sautéed
fritto, alla griglia, saltato *(free-tto, al-lah greel-ya, sal-taa-to)*

POULTRY
POLLAME *(pol-la-may)*

chicken
pollo *(pohl-lo)*

stuffed roast chicken
pollo arrosto ripieno *(pohl-lo ar-ros-to reep-yay-no)*

duck
anatra *(aa-na-tra)*

goose
oca *(o-ka)*

roasted, fried, grilled
arrosto, fritto, alla griglia *(ar-ros-to, free-tto, al-lah greel-ya)*

MEAT
CARNE *(kar-nay)*

veal
vitello *(vee-tehl-lo)*

mutton, lamb
montone, agnello *(mon-to-nay, an-yeh-llo)*

beef
manzo *(mand-zo)*

pork
maiale *(ma-ee-aa-lay)*

sausage
salsiccia *(sal-seet-chay)*

venison
carne di cervo *(kar-nay dee cher-voh)*

cured ham
prosciutto crudo *(pro-shoot-to kroo-do)*

smoked ham
prosciutto affumicato *(pro-shoot-to a-ffoo-mee-kaa-to)*

meat balls/cakes
polpette *(pol-pet-tay)*

well-done, medium, rare
ben cotto, a mezza cottura, al sangue *(behn kot-to, ah met-za kot-too-ra, al san-way)*

boiled, stewed
bollito, in umido *(boll-ee-to, in oo-mee-do)*

beef stew
stracotto (di manzo) (*stra-kot-to [dee mand-zo]*)

brawn
soppressata
(sop-preh-ssaa-ta)

platter of cold meats
piatto da portata di affettati
(pee-atto da por-taa-ta dee a-ffeh-ttaa-tee)

salami
salame *(sa-laa-may)*

pork – smoked
maiale affumicato
(ma-ee-aa-lay a-ffoo-mee-kaa-to)

bacon – smoked
pancetta affumicata
(pan-chet-ta a-ffoo-mee-kaa-to)

rice with peas
risotto con piselli *(ree-sot-to kon pee-sel-lee)*

dumplings with polenta
suricitti
(soo-ree-cheet-tee)

dumplings with cheese and egg
strangolapreti
(stran-go-la-pray-tee)

pasta made with cottage cheese
pasta con ricotta
(pas-ta kon ree-kot-ta)

pasta and chick peas
pasta e ceci
(pas-ta eh chay-chee)

Vegetables, Salad and Fruit
Verdure, Insalata e Frutta *(vair-doo-ray, een-sa-laa-ta eh froo-tta)*

green cabbage
verza *(ver-tza)*

cabbage
cavolo *(ka-voh-lo)*

cauliflower
cavolfiore *(ka-vol-fyo-ray)*

carrots
carote *(ka-ro-tay)*

leek
porro (*pohr-ro)*

asparagus
asparagi *(as-pa-ra-jee)*

mushrooms
funghi *(foon-gee)*

peppers
peperoni *(pe-pe-ro-nee)*

pumpkin
zucca *(tzoo-ka)*

potatoes – boiled, fried, mashed
patate – bollite, fritte, purè *(pa-tah-tay – boh-lee-tay, free-tay, poo-ray)*

lettuce
lattuga *(la-ttoo-ga)*

beetroot
barbabietola *(bar-ba-bya-to-la)*

cucumber
cetriolo *(che-tree-o-lo)*

tomato
pomodoro *(po-moh-doh-ro)*

root celery
sedano *(say-da-no)*

green beans
fagiolini *(fa-jo-lee-nee)*

apples
mele *(may-lay)*

pears
pere *(pair-ay)*

bananas
banane *(ba-naa-nay)*

pineapple
ananas *(aa-na-nas)*

apricots
albicocche *(al-bee-ko-chay)*

peaches
pesche *(pes-kay)*

blueberries
mirtilli *(meer-tee-llee)*

strawberries
fragole *(fraa-go-lay)*

raspberries
lamponi *(lam-po-nee)*

redcurrants
ribes *(ree-bes)*

blackcurrants
ribes nero *(ree-bes neh-ro)*

plums
susine *(soo-see-nay)*

fruit salad
macedonia *(ma-kay-do-nee-a)*

DESSERTS & CAKES
DOLCI & TORTE

jelly
gelatina *(je-la-tee-na)*

apple pie
torta di mele
(tohr-ta dee may-lay)

chocolate cake
torta di cioccolato *(tohr-ta dee chok-ko-la-to)*

sponge cake with custard and cream
zuppa inglese
(tsoop-pa eeng-lay-say)

sponge cake with cream cheese, chocolate and candied fruit
cassata siciliana *(ka-saa-ta see-chee-lee-a-na)*

sponge cake with mascarpone, eggs and chocolate
tiramisù
(tee-ra-mee-soo)

soufflé with ricotta and candied fruit
budino di ricotta *(boo-dee-no dee ree-ko-tta)*

chestnut cake with sultanas, pine nuts
castagnaccio
(kas-tan-ya-cho)

cinnamon custard
lattaiolo *(lat-ta-yo-lo)*

biscuits
biscotti *(bees-ko-tee)*

Christmas sponge cake
pandoro *(pan-doh-ro)*

Christmas bread with candied fruit
panettone
(pa-neh-tto-nay)

nut and honey cake
pangiallo *(pan-gee-a-llo)*

Italian blancmange and crème brûlée
panna cotta
(pahn-nah kot-ta)

rich fruit cake with figs and honey
pestingolo
(pes-teen-go-lo)

layered cake with meringue, fresh fruit and whipped cream
torta margherita
(tohr-ta mar-gay-ree-ta)

MONEY AND SHOPPING

MONEY MATTERS 59
AFFARI DI DENARO 59

POST OFFICE 59
UFFICIO POSTALE 59

SHOPPING 60
FARE COMPERE 60

BUYING CLOTHES 61
COMPRARE VESTIARIO 61

GROCERY SHOPPING 61
COMPERE DI DROGHERIA 61

CLOTHING SIZES 63
TAGLIE 63

MONEY MATTERS
AFFARI DI DENARO

bureau de change
cambiavalute/cambio
(kam-bee-a-va-loo-teh/ kam-bee-o)

cash dispenser/ATM
cassa automatica/ bancomat *(kas-sa ow-to-ma-tee-ka/ban-ko-mat)*

Where can I change money?
Dove posso cambiare denaro?
(do-veh pos-so kam-bee-aa-ray de-naa-ro)

Where is ...?
Dov'è ...? *(do-veh)*

- **an ATM, a cash machine, a bank**
- il bancomat, la cassa automatica, una banca *(eel ban-ko-mat, la kas-sa ow-to-ma-tee-ka, oo-na ban-ka)*

When does the bank open/close?
Quando apre/chiude la banca? *(kwan-do a-pray/ kee-oo-day la ban-ka)*

How much commission do you charge?
Quanto prendete di commissione?
(kwan-to pren-deh-teh dee ko-mee-see-o-ne)

I want to ...
Voglio/vorrei ...
(vol-yo/ vor-reh-ee ...)

- **cash a traveller's cheque**
- riscuotere un assegno di viaggio *(rees-kwo-tere oon a-ssen-yo dee vee-a-jo)*

- **change £50**
- cambiare cinquanta sterline *(kam-bee-a-ray chin-kwan-ta stayr-lee-nay)*

- **make a transfer**
- trasferire soldi *(tras-fer-ee-ray sol-dee)*

POST OFFICE
UFFICIO POSTALE

How much is ...?
Quanto costa ...?
(kwan-to kos-ta)

- **a letter to ...**
- una lettera per ...
  (oo-na let-te-rah pehr)

- **a small parcel to ...**
- un pacchetto per ...
  (oon pa-ket-to pehr)

Where can I buy stamps?
Dove posso comperare dei francobolli? *(do-veh pos-so kom-pe-ra-ray day fran-ko-bol-lee)*

SHOPPING
FARE COMPERE

What does it cost?
Quanto costa?
(kwan-to kos-ta)

What is the total?
Quant'è in tutto?
(kwan-tay in too-tto)

Where do I pay?
Dove si paga?
(do-veh see pa-ja)

I need a receipt
Ho bisogno di una ricevuta *(o bee-soy-no dee oo-na ree-ce-voo-ta)*

Do you accept credit cards?
Accetta carte di credito?
(a-chet-tah kaar-te dee kre-dee-to)

Do you take traveller's cheques?
Accetta assegni di viaggio? *(a-chet-tah a-ssen-yee dee vee-a-jo)*

Do you need a deposit?
Debbo pagare un deposito in anticipo?
(dehb-boh pa-jaa-ray oon deh-po-see-toh in an-tee-chee-po)

Can you wrap it up for me?
Può farmi un pacchetto regalo? *(pwo faar-mi oon pa-ketto re-gaa-lo)*

VAT
I.V.A. (imposta sul valore aggiunto)
(eem-pos-ta sool va-lo-ray a-jee-oon-to)

This is not what I want
Non è quello che voglio
(non eh kway-llo kay vo-lee-o)

This isn't correct (bill)
Questo è sbagliato
(kwes-to eh zbal-yaa-to)

I want my money back
Voglio un rimborso *(vol-yo oon reem-bor-so)*

This is ...
Questo è ... *(kwes-to eh)*

- **broken**
- rotto *(roht-to)*

- **damaged**
- guasto *(gwaas-to)*

BUYING CLOTHES
COMPRARE VESTIARIO

Can I try this on?
Posso provarlo?
(pos-so pro-vaar-lo)

It is too ...
E' troppo *(eh troh-po)*

- **big**
- grande *(gran-day)*

- **small**
- piccolo *(pee-ko-lo)*

- **tight**
- stretto *(stre-ttoh)*

- **wide**
- largo *(laar-goh)*

- **expensive**
- caro *(kaa-ro)*

- **fragile, delicate**
- fragile, delicato *(fra-jee-le, de-lee-ka-to)*

I'll take ...
Prendo ...*(pren-doh ...)*

- **this one**
- questo *(kwes-to)*

- **two**
- due *(doo-e)*

GROCERY SHOPPING
COMPERE DI DROGHERIA

Where can I buy ...?
Dove posso comperare ...?
(do-veh pos-so kom-pe-ra-ray)

- **bread**
- pane *(paa-neh)*

- **rolls**
- panini *(pa-nee-nee)*

- **cake**
- torta *(tohr-tah)*

- **cheese**
- formaggio *(for-ma-jee-o)*

- **butter**
- burro *(boo-rro)*

- **milk**
- latte *(laat-tay)*

- **water**
- acqua minerale *(ak-wa mee-ne-ra-le)*

- **wine**
- vino *(vee-no)*

- **sparkling wine**
- vino frizzante *(vee-no free-saan-te)*

- **beer**
- birra *(bee-rra)*

- **fruit juice**
- succo di frutta *(soo-ko dee froo-tta)*

- **meat**
- carne *(kaar-ne)*

- **ham**
- prosciutto *(pro-shoo-tto)*

- **polony, cold meats**
- mortadella, salumi *(mor-tah-day-la, sa-loo-mee)*

- **fruit**
- frutta *(froo-tta)*

- **vegetables**
- verdure *(ver-doo-re)*

- **eggs**
- uova *(wo-va)*

I'll take ...
Prendo ... *(pren-doh ...)*

- **one kilo**
- un chilo *(oon kee-lo)*

- **three slices**
- tre fette *(treh fet-teh)*

- **a portion of**
- una porzione di *(oo-na port-see-o-ne dee)*

- **a packet of**
- un pacchetto di *(oon pa-ket-to dee)*

- **a can/tin of**
- una scatola di *(oo-na ska-to-lah dee)*

- **a bottle of**
- una bottiglia di *(oo-na bo-tteel-ya dee)*

CLOTHING SIZES - TAGLIE

Women's Wear - Abbigliamento femminile

UK	Cont. Europe	USA
10	**36**	**8**
12	**38**	**10**
14	**40**	**12**
16	**42**	**14**
18	**44**	**16**

Menswear - Abbigliamento maschile

UK	Cont. Europe	USA
36	**46**	**36**
38	**48**	**38**
40	**50**	**40**
42	**52**	**42**
44	**54**	**44**
46	**56**	**46**

Men's Shirts - Camicie da uomo

UK	Cont. Europe	USA
14	**36**	**14**
14.5	**37**	**14.5**
15	**38**	**15**
15.5	**39**	**15.5**
16	**40**	**16**
17	**42**	**17**

Shoes - Scarpe

UK	Cont. Europe	USA
5	**38**	**6**
6	**39**	**7**
7	**41**	**8**
8	**42**	**9**
9	**43**	**10**
10	**44**	**11**
11	**45**	**12**

SIGHTSEEING 65
GIRI TURISTICI 65

ENTERTAINMENT 66
DIVERTIMENTO 66

SPORT 67
SPORT 67

SIGHTSEEING
GIRI TURISTICI

Tourist Office
Ufficio turistico *(oo-fee-chee-o too-rees-tee-ko)*

Do you have brochures/leaflets?
Avete degli opuscoli?
(a-ve-teh day-lee o-poos-ko-lee)

I/We want to visit ...
Voglio/vogliamo visitare ...
(vol-yo/vol-yee-a-mo vee-see-ta-ray)

When is it open/ closed?
Quando apre/chiude?
(kwan-do a-pray/kee-oo-day)

What does it cost?
Quanto costa?
(kwan-to kos-ta)

Are there any reductions for ...?
Ci sono riduzioni/tariffe speciali per ...? *(chee so-no ree-doo-tsee-o-nee/ ta-ree-fay spe-kee-ah-lee pehr)*

- **children**
- bambini
  (bam-bee-nee)

- **senior citizens**
- anziani
  (ant-see-a-nee)

- **students**
- studenti
  (stoo-den-tee)

Are there any tours?
Ci sono delle visite turistiche? *(chee so-no day-la vee-see-teh too-ree-stee-ke)*

Where/when does the coach/bus depart/return?
Da dove/quando parte/ritorna il pullman?
(dah do-veh/kwan-do par-tay/ree-tor-na eel poolman)

Where is the museum?
Dov'è il museo?
(do-veh eel moo-se-o)

How much is the entrance fee?
Quanto costa l'entrata?
(kwan-to kos-ta len-traa-ta)

ENTERTAINMENT
DIVERTIMENTO

Is there a list of cultural events?
C'è una lista degli eventi culturali? *(che oo-na lees-ta day-lee e-ven-tee kool-too-raa-lee)*

Are there any festivals?
Ci sono dei festival? *(chee so-no day fes-tee-val)*

I would like to go to ...
Vorrei andare ...
(vor-re-hee aan-da-ray ...)

- **the theatre**
- al teatro *(al tee-a-tro)*

- **the opera**
- all'opera *(all-o-pe-rah)*

- **the ballet**
- al balletto *(al bal-leh-tto)*

- **the cinema/movies**
- al cinema *(al chee-ne-ma)*

- **a concert**
- un concerto *(oon kon-cher-to)*

Do I have to book?
Bisogna prenotare? *(bi-son-ya pre-no-taa-ray)*

How much are the tickets?
Quanto costano i biglietti? *(kwan-to kos-taa-no ee beel-yay-ttee)*

Two tickets for ...
Due biglietti per ... *(doo-ay beel-yay-ttee pehr ...)*

- **tonight**
- questa sera *(kwes-ta seh-ra)*

- **tomorrow night**
- domani sera *(do-maa-nee seh-ra)*

- **the early show**
- lo spettacolo del pome riggio *(lo spe-ttaa-ko-loh del po-me-ree-jo)*

- **late show**
- spettacolo serale *(spe-ttaa-ko-loh se-ra-lay)*

When does the performance start/end?
Quando incomincia/finisce lo spettacolo? *(kwan-do een-ko-meen-cha/fee-nee-shay lo spe-ttaa-ko-loh)*

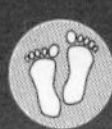

Where is ...?
Dov'è ...? *(do-veh)*

- **a good bar**
- un buon bar *(oon bwon bar)*

- **good live music**
- una buona orchestra *(oo-na bwo-na or-kes-tra)*

Is it ...?
È ...? *(eh)*

- **expensive**
- caro *(ka-ro)*

- **noisy**
- rumoroso *(roo-mo-ro-so)*

- **crowded**
- affollato *(a-ffo-llaa-to)*

How do I get there?
Come ci si arriva? *(ko-may chee see a-rree-va)*

SPORT
SPORT

Where can we ...?
Dove possiamo ...? *(do-veh po-ssee-a-mo)*

- **play tennis/golf**
- giocare a tennis/golf *(jee-o-kaa-ray ah tennis/golf)*

- **go skiing**
- sciare *(shee-a-ray)*

- **go swimming**
- nuotare *(nwo-taa-ray)*

- **go fishing**
- pescare *(pe-shaa-ray)*

- **go riding**
- andare a cavallo *(aan-da-ray ah ka-val-lo)*

- **go cycling**
- andare in bicicletta *(aan-da-ray in bee-chee-klet-te)*

- **hire bicycles**
- noleggiare biciclette *(no-lay-djaa-ray bee-chee-klet-te)*

- **hire tackle**
- noleggiare articoli per la pesca *(no-lay-djaa-ray ar-tee-ko-lee pehr la pe-sha)*

- **hire golf clubs**
- noleggiare mazze da golf *(no-lay-djaa-ray mat-seh da golf)*

- **hire skis**
- noleggiare sci *(no-lay-djaa-ray shee)*

- **hire a boat**
- noleggiare una barca *(no-lay-djaa-ray oo-na bar-ka)*

- **hire skates**
- noleggiare pattini *(no-lay-djaa-ray pa-ttee-nee)*

- **hire an umbrella**
- noleggiare un ombrello *(no-lay-djaa-ray oon om-breh-llo)*

- **hire a deck chair**
- noleggiare una sedia a sdraio *(no-lay-djaa-ray oo-na se-dee-a ah sdraa-ee-o)*

How much is it ...?
Quanto costa ...? *(kwan-to kos-ta)*

- **per hour**
- all'ora *(a-llo-rah)*

- **per day**
- al giorno *(al jor-no)*

- **per session/game**
- alla partita *(al-la par-tee-ta)*

Is it ...?
È ...? *(eh)*

- **safe**
- sicuro *(see-koo-ro)*

- **deep**
- profondo *(pro-fon-doh)*

- **clean**
- pulito *(poo-lee-to)*

How do we get there?
Come ci si arriva? *(ko-may chee see a-rree-va)*

no swimming/diving
vietato nuotare/tuffarsi *(vee-ay-ta-to nwo-ta-ray/too-ffar-see)*

Are there currents?
Ci sono correnti? *(chee so-no co-rren-tee)*

Do I need a fishing permit?
Ho bisogno di un permesso per la pesca? *(o bee-son-yo dee oon per-meh-sso pehr la pe-sha)*

Where can I get one?
Dove posso trovarlo? *(do-veh pos-so tro-vaar-loh)*

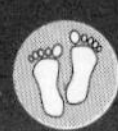

Is there a guide for walks?
C'è una guida per le escursioni a piedi? *(che oo-na gwee-da pehr lay es-koor-see-o-nee ah pee-ay-dee)*

Do I need walking boots?
Ho bisogno di scarponi speciali? *(o bee-son-yo dee skar-po-nee spe-kee-a-lee)*

How much is a ski pass?
Quanto costa una tessera per sciare? *(kwan-to kos-ta oo-na te-sse-rah pehr shee-a-ray)*

Is it safe to ski today?
È sicuro sciare oggi? *(eh see-koo-ro shee-a-ray o-jee)*

I'm a beginner
Sono un principiante *(so-no oon preen-chee-pee-an-te)*

Which is an easy run?
Quale è una pista facile? *(kwa-le eh oo-na pees-ta fa-chee-le)*

My skis are too long/short
Questi sci sono troppo lunghi/corti *(kwes-tee schee so-no troh-ppo loon-gee/kor-tee)*

run closed
pista chiusa *(pees-ta kee-oo-sa)*

avalanches
valanghe *(va-lang-geh)*

We want to go ...
Noi vogliamo andare a ... *(noy vol-yee-a-mo aan-da-ray ah ...)*

- **hiking**
- fare escursionismo a piedi *(faa-ray es-koor-see-o-nees-mo ah pee-ay-dee*

- **sailing**
- fare vela *(faa-ray veh-lah)*

- **ice-skating**
- pattinare su ghiaccio *(pa-ttee-na-ray soo gee-a-cho)*

- **water-skiing**
- fare lo sci acquatico *(faa-ray lo shee ak-wa-tee-ko)*

PHARMACY/CHEMIST 71
FARMACIA 71

DOCTOR 72
DOTTORE 72

HOSPITAL 72
OSPEDALE 72

POLICE 73
LA POLIZIA 73

EMERGENCIES 73
EMERGENZE 73

FIRE DEPARTMENT 74
CORPO DEI VIGILI DEL FUOCO 74

THE HUMAN BODY 75
IL CORPO UMANO 75

PHARMACY/ CHEMIST
FARMACIA

Chains for toiletries, etc. and some medicines not on prescription
Articoli da toilette e senza ricetta medicina
(ar-tee-ko-lee da toy-let-te eh sen-sa ree-chet-ta me-dee-chee-na)

health shop
il negozio di cibi naturali
(eel ne-got-see-o dee chee-bee na-too-raa-lee)

Have you got something for ...?
Avete qualche rimedio per ...? *(a-veh-teh kwal-ke ree-me-dee-o pehr ...)*

- **car sickness**
- il mal d'auto *(eel mal dow-to)*

- **diarrhoea**
- la diarrea *(la dee-ay-rrea)*

- **a headache**
- il mal di testa *(eel mal dee tes-tah)*

- **a sore throat**
- il mal di gola *(eel mat dee goh-lah)*

- **stomachache**
- il mal di stomaco *(eel mal dee sto-maa-ko)*

- **a cold or flu**
- raffreddore o l'influenza *(raff-re-ddo-reh o leen-floo-en-sa)*

I need ...
Ho bisogno di ...
(o bee-son-yo dee ...)

- **indigestion tablets**
- pillole per indigestione *(peel-lo-le pehr een-dee-ges-tee-o-ne)*

- **laxative**
- lassativo *(las-saa-tee-vo)*

- **sleeping tablets**
- pillole per dormire *(peel-lo-le pehr dor-mee-ray)*

- **a painkiller**
- un analgesico *(oon an-al-je-see-ko)*

Is it safe for children?
Va bene per bambini?
(vah be-nay pehr bam-bee-nee)

I'm a diabetic
Sono diabetico/a *(so-no dee-a-be-tee-ko/a*

I'm pregnant
Sono incinta
(so-no een-cheen-ta)

allergic
allergico/a *(aller-jee-ko/a)*

DOCTOR
DOTTORE

I am ill
Sono ammalato/a
(so-no am-ma-laa-to/a)

I need a doctor
Ho bisogno di un dottore
(o bee-son-yo dee oon do-tto-reh)

He/she has high temperature
Lui/lei ha la febbre alta
(loo-ee/lay a la feb-bray al-tah)

It hurts
Fa male *(fa maa-leh)*

I'm going to be sick!
Ho voglia di vomitare!
(o vol-yo dee vo-mee-taa-ray)

Dentist
il/la dentista
(eel/la den-tees-ta)

I have toothache
Ho mal di denti
(o mal dee den-tee)

Ophthalmologist
l'oftalmologo/a
(lof-tal-moh-lo-jo/a)

HOSPITAL
OSPEDALE

Will I have to go to hospital?
Debbo andare all'ospedale?
(deb-boh an-daa-ray al-los-pe-daa-lay)

Where is the hospital?
Dov'è l'ospedale?
(do-veh los-pe-daa-lay)

Which ward?
Quale sala?
(kwaa-le saa-la)

When are visiting hours?
Quando sono le ore di visita? *(kwan-do so-no le o-ray vee-see-ta)*

Where is casualty?
Dov'è il pronto soccorso?
(do-veh eel pron-to so-kkor-soh)

POLICE
LA POLIZIA

Call the police
Chiami la polizia *(kee-aa-mee la po-leet-see-a)*

I have been robbed
Sono stato derubato *(so-no sta-to de-roo-baa-to)*

My car has been stolen
La mia macchina è stata rubata
(la mee-a ma-kkee-na eh sta-ta roo-baa-ta)

My car has been broken into
Hanno rubato nella mia macchina
(an-no roo-baa-to nella mee-a ma-kkee-na)

I have been attacked
Sono stato assalito *(so-no sta-to ass-al-eet-o)*

I want to report a theft
Voglio denunciare un furto *(vol-yo de-noon-chee-a-ray oon foor-to)*

Where is the police station?
Dov'è la stazione di polizia? *(do-veh la sta-tsy-o-ne dee po-leet-see-a)*

EMERGENCIES
EMERGENZE

Call an ambulance!
Chiami un'ambulanza!
(kee-aa-mee oon-am-boo-lant-sa)

There's been an accident
C'è stato un incidente
(cheh sta-to oon een-chee-den-te)

Someone is injured
C'è un ferito *(cheh oon fe-ree-to)*

Hurry up!
Presto! *(pres-toh)*

Help!
Aiuto! *(a-ee-oo-to)*

Could you please help me?
Per favore, mi aiuti?
(pehr fa-vo-ray, mee a-ee-oo-tee)

My son/daughter is missing
Mio figlio/figlia è smarrita
(mee-o/mee-a fee-lee-yo/fee-lee-ya eh sma-rree-ta)

This is an emergency!
C'è un'emergenza!
(cheh oon-em-er-gen-sa)

I need a report for my insurance
Devo avere un rapporto per la mia assicurazione
(day-vo a-veh-reh oon rap-po-roh pehr la mee-a a-ssee-koo-rat-see-o-nay)

I want to phone my embassy
Voglio telefonare alla mia ambasciata
(vol-yo tay-lay-fo-naa-re al-lah mee-a am-ba-sshee-a-ta)

I am lost
Sono perduto
(so-no per-doo-to)

FIRE DEPARTMENT
CORPO DEI VIGILI DEL FUOCO

Fire!
Fuoco!
(fwo-ko)

Look out!
Attenzione!
(a-tten-see-o-nay)

Call the fire department
Chiami i vigili del fuoco
(kee-aa-mee ee vee-jee-lee del fwo-ko)

The address is ...
L'indirizzo è ...
(leen-dee-ree-tso eh ...)

I need ...
Ho bisogno di ...
(o bee-son-yo dee ...)

- **a fire extinguisher**
- un estintore
(oon es-teen-to-re)

- **medical assistance**
- assistenza medica
(a-ssees-tent-sa me-dee-cha)

THE HUMAN BODY
IL CORPO UMANO

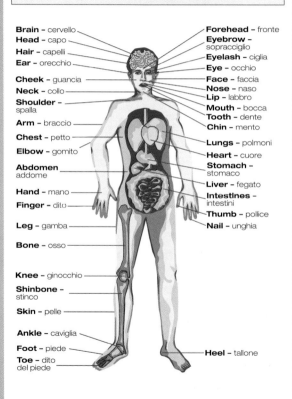

Brain – cervello
Head – capo
Hair – capelli
Ear – orecchio
Cheek – guancia
Neck – collo
Shoulder – spalla
Arm – braccio
Chest – petto
Elbow – gomito
Abdomen addome
Hand – mano
Finger – dito
Leg – gamba
Bone – osso
Knee – ginocchio
Shinbone – stinco
Skin – pelle
Ankle – caviglia
Foot – piede
Toe – dito del piede

Forehead – fronte
Eyebrow – sopracciglio
Eyelash – ciglia
Eye – occhio
Face – faccia
Nose – naso
Lip – labbro
Mouth – bocca
Tooth – dente
Chin – mento
Lungs – polmoni
Heart – cuore
Stomach – stomaco
Liver – fegato
Intestines – intestini
Thumb – pollice
Nail – unghia
Heel – tallone

FORMS OF ADDRESS 77
FORME PER RIVOLGERSI A QUALCUNO 77

MANNERS 78
MANIERE 78

APPROPRIATE DRESS 78
ABITO ADATTO 78

COMMUNICATION 80
COMUNICAZIONI 80

HIERARCHY AND RESPECT 81
ORDINE DI PRECEDENZA E RISPETTO 81

DINING FORMALITIES 82
FORMALITÀ DI PRANZARE 82

FORMS OF ADDRESS

FORME PER RIVOLGERSI A QUALCUNO

Signorina (Miss) is rarely used in Italy today and is best avoided, unless a woman appears relatively young and you are unsure of her marital status. Generally speaking, *Signore* (for a man) and *Signora* (for a woman) are the safest options. A male university graduate is given the title of *Dottore*, and *Dottoressa* is the female equivalent. If you need to call a waiter, use the word *senta*, which means 'please come here'.

Frequent and vigorous handshakes can be common on social occasions. Upon arrival and departure, shake hands with everyone individually in a group, as one general 'hello' or 'goodbye' to the group will not really be appreciated. Italians will not hesitate to greet people they know with an embrace, usually kissing each other once on each cheek – this applies to both males and females.

In stores or restaurants, it is a courtesy to greet people with an appropriate greeting when you arrive and when you leave. *Buon giorno* on arrival and *arrivederci* as you leave are the appropriate greetings.

MANNERS

MANIERE

Younger people should give up their seats to older people on public transport. Chewing, leaning and slouching are unacceptable in public, and you should also avoid raising your hand or fingers. On the other hand, gentle pushing and shoving in queues is a common occurrence in Italy.

Some typically Italian gestures may need to be explained. Touching your nose indicates confidentiality. Pointing with the index and little finger is a gesture used when wishing someone bad luck. Placing the hand on the stomach indicates dislike for someone. Slapping your raised arm above the elbow and thumbing your nose are both considered to be very offensive gestures.

APPROPRIATE DRESS

ABITO ADATTO

It is important to know what to wear in a business environment. Men should wear tailored dark suits and sophisticated ties - quality fabrics such as lightweight wools and silks are customary. Cuff links add to the

sophistication, as do tie clips and watches. Italians generally use aftershaves of the highest quality, but not too much.

Women are advised to dress for business with elegant simplicity, and to accessorize with jewellery. Darker, subdued shades are most commonly worn, with brighter colours used for accessories. Perfumes are very popular. It is fashionable, especially in summer, for women not to wear stockings.

Although leisure wear is less formal, shorts are unacceptable in public and you will not be allowed into a church if you are wearing shorts or a sleeveless top. On the street, jeans and sneakers are accepted as leisure wear, although this kind of clothing is mainly for the gym or the beach.

When it comes to social occasions, your clothing will be perceived as a reflection of your social standing and relative success. Informal dress does not exist in Italy, so even if you receive an invitation stating 'informal' dress, do not embarrass yourself by arriving in sweatpants and a T-shirt. 'Informal' means tastefully coordinated clothes, including a jacket and tie. An invitation stating 'formal' would mean that you should don your very best dressy evening wear.

Clothes should always be stylish, chosen with good taste and not be gaudy. Quality and labels are important factors as the Italians are very fashion-conscious. Dark, discreet colours in the best fabrics - like silk - are the way to go.

COMMUNICATION

COMUNICAZIONI

Italian communication is highly emotive, eloquent and tends to be very animated, so expect to be interrupted!

Communication tends to be quieter in a business setting The authority figure will not have to raise his or her voice as this is an individual who is used to being noticed and listened to.

Trust is very important to Italians. This is why they prefer to do business with people they have already met. First impressions are also important, so be sure to make eye contact immediately when being introduced to someone. Italians show their interest with sustained eye contact.

In Italian culture, people are traditionally expected to behave with a sense of decorum and formality at all times. This concept is known as *Bella Figura* ('beautiful figure'), which generally means presenting yourself well, especially when communicating.

HIERARCHY AND RESPECT

ORDINE DI PRECEDENZA E RISPETTO

A person's position and influence within an organization, as well as their achievements, are of great importance to Italians. Both in a business environment and in family life, a hierarchical structure is strictly adhered to. Much respect is given to those higher in command and age.

Although women generally receive a lot of respect from men in Italy, they are still not given equal rights and similar positions when it comes to business.

Italians are a proud nation. Never insult an Italian's honour or that of his or her friends and family. Also don't make any negative remarks about the area in which they live. That said, Italians are usually responsive to constructive criticism, as long as it is presented in such a way that they are able to retain their pride and dignity.

Italians very rarely speak to each other on a first-name basis in business, so only use their Christian name if you have been told to do so. Complementing employees in public is definitely not standard procedure.

Punctuality is appreciated for business meetings, but you should not be offended if you are kept waiting by your host. Make sure you always close doors behind you and knock before entering.

Religion is a very important part of life in Italy, so make sure that you never blaspheme and swear.

DINING FORMALITIES

FORMALITÀ DI PRANZARE

Behaving incorrectly when having a business lunch could have serious consequences regarding your business deal. You will be thought to be impolite if you leave the table during the meal unless absolutely necessary, even if you are going to the toilet.

The person who is perceived to be the most important is usually seated to the right

of the host and at the center of the side of the table. It is quite common for couples to be spilt up - this is done to help improve conversation among those people who have not met each other before.

If you are the person who has invited your business associates for a meal, you should collect the bill.

Wines are sipped at leisure and for the purpose of enjoyment, not for getting drunk. You will seldom find Italians getting drunk.

If you are offered more food than you wish to consume, you can decline politely, but you may have to be prepared to insist. Italians are very generous when it comes to their food and you might not be believed when you say you have had enough.

In Italy it is offensive to raise your fingers or hands to gain the waiter's attention. The best way is to make eye contact with him or gesture with your palm facing the floor.

When invited to a meal at someone's home, it is appropriate to bring a gift like chocolates or flowers for the hostess. It is also a good idea to follow up with a phone call the next day.

OFFICIAL HOLIDAYS 85
FESTE UFFICIALI 85

REGIONAL HOLIDAYS 86
FESTE REGIONALI 86

NATIONAL DAY 86
GIORNATA NAZIONALE 86

SPECIAL FESTIVALS 86
FESTIVAL SPECIALI 86

OFFICIAL HOLIDAYS
FESTE UFFICIALI

New Year's Day
Capodanno or *Primo dell'Anno* (1 January)
Great festivities are held throughout Italy.

Epiphany
Epifania (6 January)
A religious holiday.

Easter Monday
Lunedì di Pasqua
The day after Easter is spent with the family decorating and eating hard-boiled eggs, as well as chocolate eggs and traditional Easter cake (*Colomba Pasquale*), a sponge cake in the shape of a dove representing peace and harmony.

Liberation Day
Anniversario della Liberazione (25 April)
A public holiday celebrating the liberation of Italy in 1945.

Labour Day
Festa del Lavoro (1 May)
A day off for workers.

Assumption Day
Ferragosto (15 August)
A religious holiday.

All Saints' Day
Ognissanti (1 November)
A religious holiday in honour of the saints.

Immaculate Conception
L'immacolata Concezione (8 December)
A religious holiday.

Christmas Day
Natale (25 December)
Celebrated with church services and the giving of gifts.

St Stephen's Day
Santo Stefano (26 December)
The day after Christmas is a public holiday, usually spent with the family.

REGIONAL HOLIDAYS
FESTE REGIONALI

Each region, town and village in Italy has its own holiday and annual festival. These festivals are usually in summer and are held in honour of the local patron saint.

NATIONAL DAY
GIORNATA NAZIONALE

Anniversary of the Republic *Festa della Repubblica* (2 June)
Italy's National Day.

SPECIAL FESTIVALS
FESTIVAL SPECIALI

Carnevale
Carnival is a joyous celebration consisting of various kinds of merrymaking and festivities. It takes place throughout the country during the last few days before the commencement of the austere 40 days of Lent, which precedes Easter in the Christian calendar.

il Palio di Siena
(usually on 26 August)
Siena's Palio starts with a grand historical parade of people in medieval costumes. This takes place in the *Campo* (main square) of Siena. The festival closes with a reckless bareback horse race around the square in which the 17 different districts of the town compete for the final prize, the *palio* - a prestigious hand-painted banner.

Stagione Lirica del l'arena di Verona
(July to August)
This is Verona's annual open-air opera festival. Various operas are performed on the enormous stage of the Arena - a Roman Amphitheatre. The arena is so big that live elephants can be used on stage for performances of Verdi's *Aïda*.

Ferragosto
(August holidays)
Centred around the 15th of August, this holiday period at the height of summer is observed nationally. All factories close down and everyone goes on holiday to the seaside, to the mountains and to the lakes. Roads are congested during this period and holiday resorts are usually very crowded.

A

abbey abbazia **f**
abortion aborto **m**
about (approximately) circa
above sopra
abroad all'estero
abscess ascesso **m**
absolutely assolutamente
accelerator acceleratore **m**
accent accento **m**
accept accettare
accident incidente **m**
accommodation alloggio **m**
account conto **m**
accurate preciso/a
ache dolore **m**
adapter adattatore **m**
adhesive tape nastro adesivo **m**
admission fee quota d'entrata
adult (adj, n) adulto/a **m/f**
advance, in advance anticipo **m,** anticipatamente
advert, advertisement pubblicità **f**
advise avvisare
aeroplane aeroplano **m**
afraid, afraid of paura, paura di
after dopo
afternoon pomeriggio **m**
afterwards in seguito
again di nuovo
against contro
age età **f**
ago, a week ago fa, una settimana fa
agree accordarsi
agreement accordo **m**
air aria **f**
air conditioning aria condizionata
air ticket biglietto aereo **m**
airmail posta aerea **f**
airport aeroporto **m**
aisle corridoio **m**
aisle seat posto sul corridoio
all right va bene
allow permettere
almond mandorla **f**
almost quasi
alone solo
already già
also anche
although benchè, sebbene
altogether in tutto
always sempre
a.m. (before noon) antimeridiane, del mattino
am, I am sono, io sono
amazing incredibile
amber ambra **f**

ENGLISH → ITALIAN

ambulance ambulanza **f**
among tra
amount quantità **f**
anaesthetic anestesia **f**
ancient antico/a
and e
angry arrabbiato/a
animal animale **m**
ankle caviglia **f**
anniversary anniversario **m**
annoy dare fastidio
annual annuale
another un altro
answer risposta **f**
ant formica **f**
antacid antiacido
anybody chiunque
anything qualche cosa, qualcosa
apartment appartamento **m**
appendicitis appendicite **f**
apology scusa **f**
appointment appuntamento **m**
apron grembiule **m**
are sono
area area **f**
armchair poltrona **f**
arrange sistemare
arrest (n) arresto **m**
arrest (vb) arrestare
arrival arrivo **m**
art arte **f**
artist artista **f**
ask domandare
astonishing stupefacente
at a
attack (n) attacco **m**
attack (vb) attaccare, assalire
attic soffitta **f**
audience pubblico **m**
aunt zia **f**
auto-teller sportello automatico
autumn autunno **m**
available disponibile
avalanche valanga **f**
avenue viale **m**
average mediocre
avoid evitare
awake sveglio
away via
awful brutto/a

B

baby buggy passeggino **m**
baby food cibo per bambini, alimenti per l'infanzia
back schiena **f**
backache mal di schiena
backpack zaino **m**
bacon pancetta **f**
bad cattivo/a
bag borsa **f**
baggage bagagli **m**

ENGLISH → ITALIAN

baggage reclaim ritiro bagagli
bait esca **f**
bakery panificio **m**
balcony balcone **m**
ballpoint pen penna a sfera
Baltic Sea il mare Baltico
bandage benda **f**
bar of chocolate tavoletta di cioccolato
barber barbiere **m**
bark (n, of tree) corteccia **f**
bark (vb, dog) abbaiare
barn granaio **m**
barrel barile **m**
basement seminterrato **m**
basket cestino **m**
bath bagno **m**
bathroom camera da bagno
Bavaria Baviera
bay baia **f**
bay leaf foglia d'alloro
be essere
beach spiaggia **f**
bean fagiolo **m**
beard barba **f**
beautiful bello/a
beauty salon istituto di bellezza
because perchè
bed letto **m**
bed & breakfast camera con colazione, alloggio prima calazione
bee ape **f**
beef manzo **m**
before prima di
beginner principiante
behind dietro
Belgium Belgio **m**
believe credere
bell campanello **m**
below sotto
belt cintura **f**
bend curva **f**
beside accanto
bet (n) scommessa **f**
bet (vb) scommettere
better meglio
beyond oltre
bicycle bicicletta **f**
big grande
bill conto **m**
bin pattumiera **f,** bidone **m**
binoculars binocoli
bird uccello **m**
birth nascita **f**
birth certificate certificato di nascita
birthday compleanno **m**
birthday card biglietto di auguri di compleanno
birthday present regalo per il compleanno
biscuit biscotto **m**
bit pezzo **m**
bite (n) morso **m**
bite (vb) mordere

black nero/a
Black Forest Foresta Nera
black ice strato di ghiaccio invisibile
blackcurrants ribes neri
blanket coperta **f**
bleach decolorante **m**
bleed sanguinare
blind (adj) cieco/a
blind (n, for window) tenda veneziana **f**
blister vescica **f**
block of flats blocco di appartamenti **m**
blocked bloccato
blood sangue **m**
blood pressure pressione del sangue
blouse camicetta **f**
blow-dry asciugare con l'asciugacapelli
blue blu
blunt spuntato/a
blusher rosso per le guancie
boar cinghiale **m**
boarding card la carta d'imbarco
boarding house pensione **f**
boat nave **f**
boat trip viaggio in nave
body corpo **m**
boil (n, med) foruncolo **m**
boil (vb) bollire
bone osso **m**
bonnet (of car) cofano **m**
book (n) libro **m**
book (vb, ticket) prendere un biglietto per
bookshop libreria **f**
boot (car) portabagagli **m**
boot (shoe) stivale **m**
border frontiera **f**
boring noioso/a
born nato/a
borrow prendere a prestito
both tutti e due
bottle bottiglia **f**
bottle opener apribottiglie **m**
bottom (at the) in fondo alla
bow tie cravatta a farfalla
bowl scodella **f**
box scatola **f**
boy ragazzo **m**
boyfriend ragazzo, amico **m**
bra reggiseno **m**
bracelet braccialetto **m**
brake freno **m**
brake fluid liquido per freni
brake light luce del freno
branch (office) succursale **f**

brand (n) marca **f**
brandy cognac **m**
bread pane **m**
break rompere
break in entrata forzata
breakable fragile
breakdown (of car) guasto **m,** panna **f**
breakdown van carro attrezzi/soccorso
breakfast prima colazione
breast seno **m**
breathe respirare
breeze brezza **f**
brewery birreria **f**
brick mattone **m**
bride sposa **f**
bridegroom sposo **m**
bridge ponte **m**
briefcase cartella **f**
bright brillante
bring portare
Britain Gran Bretagna
brochure opuscolo **m**
broken rotto/a
bronchitis bronchite **f**
brooch spilla **f**
broom scopa **f**
brother fratello **m**
brother-in-law cognato **m**
brown marrone
bruise (n) livido **m**
brush spazzola **f**
Brussels Bruxelles
bucket secchio **m**
buffet car vagone ristorante
build costruire
building edificio **m**
bulb (elec) lampadina **f**
bulb (plant) bulbo **m**
bumper (car) paraurti **m**
bunch (flowers) mazzo **m**
bunch (grapes) grappolo **m**
bureau de change cambiavalute
burglar ladro/a **m/f**
burglary furto **m**
burn (n) bruciatura **f**
burn (vb) bruciare
burst scoppiare
bus autobus **m**
bus stop fermata d'autobus
bush cespuglio **m**
business affare **m**
business trip viaggio d'affari
busy occupato/a
but ma
butcher macellaio **m**
butter burro **m**
butterfly farfalla **f**
button bottone **m**
buy comprare, comperare
by da (e.g. by author), entro le (time), via (e.g. by sea)
by myself (alone) da solo

ENGLISH → ITALIAN

bypass (road) circonvallazione **f**

C

cab taxi **m,** tassì **m**
cabbage cavolo **m**
cabin cabina **f**
cable car funivia **f**
cake torta **f**
cake shop pasticceria **f**
calculator calcolatrice **f**
calf vitello **m**
call (n) chiamata **f**
call (vb) chiamare
calm calmo/a
camp (vb) campeggiare
campsite campeggio **m**
can (n, tin) latta **f,** lattina **f,** scatola **f**
can (vb, be able to) potere
can opener apriscatole **f**
Canada Canada
canal canale **m**
cancel cancellare
cancellation cancellazione
cancer cancro **m**
candle candela **f**
candy caramella **f**
canoe canoa **f**
cap berretto **m**
capital (money) capitale **m**
capital (city) capitale **f**
car macchina **f**
car ferry traghetto **m**
car hire affittare una macchina
car insurance assicurazione per la macchina
car keys chiavi per la macchina
car parts i pezzi di ricambio
car wash autolavaggio
caravan carovana **f**
caravan site campeggio per carovane **m**
carburettor carburatore **m**
card (birthday card) biglietto di auguri (per il compleanno)
cardboard cartone **m**
cardigan cardigan **m**
careful cauto/a
caretaker custode **m/f,** guardiano **m**
carpenter falegname **m**
carpet tappeto **m**
carriage carrozza **f**
carrier bag borsa (per la spesa), busta di carta
carrot carota **f**
carry portare
carry-cot lettino portatile **m**
carton scatola di cartone

ENGLISH → ITALIAN

ENGLISH → ITALIAN

case valigia **f**
cash denaro contante
cash desk cassa **f**
cash dispenser sportello automatico
cashier cassiere/a **m/f**
cassette cassetta **f**
castle castello **m**
casualty department pronto soccorso **m**
cat gatto **m**
catch prendere, acchiappare
cathedral cattedrale **f**
Catholic cattolico/a **m/f**
cauliflower cavolfiore **m**
cave grotta **f**
CD player lettore di compact
ceiling soffitto **m**
celery sedano **m**
cellar cantina **f**
cemetery cimitero **m**
Centigrade centigrado **m**
centimetre centimetro **m**
central heating riscaldamento centrale
central locking serratura automatica
centre centro **m**
century secolo **m**
certain certo/a
certainly certamente
certificate certificato **m**
chair sedia **f**
chair lift seggiovia **f**
chambermaid cameriera **f**
champagne champagne **m**
change (n, coins) spiccioli **mpl**
change (vb) cambiare
changing room camerino **m,** spogliatoio **m** (for sports)
channel canale **m**
chapel cappella **f**
charcoal carbone di legna **m**
charge caricare
charge card carta di credito
charter flight volo charter
cheap scadente, a buon mercato
cheap rate tariffa economica
cheaper a più buon mercato
check (vb) verificare
check-in fare il check-in, accettazione bagagli
cheek guancia **f**
cheering acclamazione **f**
Cheers! Salute!
cheese formaggio **m**
chef cuoco **m**
chemist farmacista **f**
cheque assegno **m**

cheque book libretto degli assegni
cheque card carta assegni
cherry ciliegia **f**
chess scacchi **m**
chest petto **m**
chest of drawers cassettone **m**
chestnut castagna **f**
chewing gum gomma da masticare
chicken pollo **m**
chicken pox varicella **f**
child bambino/a **m/f**
child car seat seggiolino per macchina
chimney camino **m**
chin mento **m**
china porcellana **f**
China Cina **f**
chips patatine fritte
chives erba cipollina
chocolate cioccolato **m**
chocolates (box of) una scatola di cioccolatini
choir coro **m**
choose scegliere
chop (n) costoletta **f**
chop (vb) tagliare (a pezzi)
Christian name nome di battesimo
Christmas Natale **m**
Christmas Eve La Vigilia di Natale
church chiesa **f**
cider sidro **m**
cigar sigaro **m**
cigarette sigaretta **f**
cigarette lighter accendino **m**
cinema cinema **m**
circle cerchio **m**
cistern cisterna **f**
citizen cittadino/a **m/f**
city città **f**
city centre il centro della città
class classe **f**
clean pulito/a
cleaning solution detergente
cleansing lotion lozione detergente
clear chiaro/a
clever intelligente
client cliente **m**
cliff scogliera **f**
climb scalare, salire, arrampicarsi
cling film carta avvolgente adesiva **f**
clinic clinica **f**
cloakroom guardaroba **f**
clock orologio **m**
close chiudere
cloth tessuto **m**
clothes vestiti **m**
clothes line corda del bucato
clothes peg molletta da bucato **f**

cloud nuvola **f**
clutch frizione **f**
coach (railway) vagone **m**
coal carbone **m**
coast costa **f**
coastguard guardia costiera
coat cappotto **m**
coat hanger gruccia **f,** attaccapanni **m,** stampella **f**
cockroach scarafaggio **m**
cocoa cacao **m**
coconut noce di cocco
cod merluzzo **m**
code codice **m**
coffee caffè **m**
coil rotolo **m**
coin moneta **f**
Coke Coca-cola **f**
colander colatoio **m,** scola pasta **f**
cold freddo/a
collapse crollare
collar colletto **m**
collarbone clavicola **f**
colleague collega
collect collezionare
collect call telefonare a carico del destinatario
cologne acqua di colonia **f**
colour colore **m**
colour blind daltonico
colour film rullino a colori
comb pettine **m**
come venire
come back ritornare
come in entrare
comedy commedia **f**
comfortable comodo/a
company compagnia **f**
compartment scompartimento **m**
compass bussola **f**
complain lamentarsi
complaint lamentela **f**
completely completamente
composer compositore **m**
compulsory obbligatorio/a
computer computer **m**
concert concerto **m**
concession concessione **f**
concussion commozione cerebrale
condition condizione **f**
condom preservativo **m**
conference conferenza **f**
confirm confermare
confirmation conferma **f**
confuse confondere
congratulations congratulazioni
connecting flight volo coincidenza
connection coincidenza **f**

conscious conscio/a
constipated stitico/a
consulate consolato **m**
contact (n) contatto **m**
contact (vb) mettere in contatto
contact lens lenti a contatto
continue continuare
contraceptive contraccettivo, anticoncezionale
contract contratto **m**
convenient comodo/a
cook (n) cuoco **m**
cook (vb) cucinare
cooker fornello **m**
cookie biscotto **m**
cooking utensils gli utensili da cucina
cool fresco/a
cool bag/box borsa termica **f**
copy copiare
cork tappo **m**
corkscrew cavatappi **m**
corner angolo **m**
correct corretto/a
corridor corridoio **m**
cost costo **m**
cot lettino **m**
cotton cotone **m**
cotton wool cotone idrofilo
couch divano **m**
couchette cuccetta **f**
cough (n) tosse **f**
cough (vb) tossire
cough mixture sciroppo per la tosse
could potrei
couldn't non potrei
counter banco **m**
country paese **m**
countryside campagna **f**
couple coppia **f**
courier service corriere
course corso **m**
cousin cugino **m**
cover charge coperto **m**
cow mucca **f**
crab granchio **m**
craft arte **f**
cramp crampo **m**
crash (vb) schiantare
crash helmet casco **m**
cream panna **f**
crèche asilo, nido **m**
credit card carta di credito
crime crimine **m**
crisps patatine fritte
crockery stoviglie **f**
cross arrabbiato/a
crossing passaggio pedonale
crossroads incrocio **m**
crossword puzzle parole crociate
crowd folla **f**
crowded affollato/a
crown corona **f**

cruise crociera **f**
crutches stampelle **f**
cry piangere
crystal cristallo **m**
cucumber cetriolo **m**
cufflinks gemelli **m**
cup tazza **f**
cupboard armadio **m**
curly riccio/a
currency valuta **f**
current (adj) corrente
current (n) corrente **f**
curtain tenda **f**
cushion cuscino **m**
custard crema pasticciera
custom usanza **f**
customer cliente **m**
customs dogana **f**
cut (n) taglio **m**
cut (vb) tagliare
cutlery posate
cycle (n) ciclo **m**
cycle track pista per biciclette
cyst ciste **f**
cystitis cistite **f**
Czech Republic Repubblica Ceca

D

daily giornaliero/a
damage (n) danno **m**
damp umido/a
dance (vb) ballare
danger pericolo **m**
dangerous pericoloso/a
dark scuro/a
date appuntamento **m**
date of birth data di nascita
dates datteri **m**
daughter figlia **f**
daughter-in-law nuora **f**
dawn alba f
day giorno **m**
dead morto/a
deaf sordo/a
deal patto **m**
dear caro/a
death morte **f**
debts debiti **m**
decaffeinated decaffeinato
December dicembre **m**
decide decidere
decision decisione **f**
deck chair sedia a sdraio
deduct dedurre
deep profondo/a
definitely sicuramente
degree (measurement) grado **m**
degree (qualification) laurea **f**
delay (n) ritardo **m**
delay (vb) ritardare
deliberately deliberatamente
delicious delizioso/a
deliver consegnare
delivery consegna **f**
Denmark Danimarca **f**

dental floss interdentale
dentist dentista **m/f**
dentures dentiera
depart partire
department sezione
department store grande magazzino **m**
departure partenza **f**
departure lounge la sala delle partenze
deposit (n) deposito **m**
deposit (vb) depositare
describe descrivere
description descrizione **f**
desk banco **m**
dessert dolce **m**
destination destinazione **f**
details particolari **m**
detergent detersivo **m**
detour deviazione **f**
develop sviluppare
diabetic (adj, n) diabetico/a **m/f**
dial (n) quadrante **m**
dialling code prefisso **m**
dialling tone segnale di linea libera
diamond diamante **m**
diaper pannolino **m**
diarrhoea diarrea **f**
diary agenda **f**
dice dado **m**
dictionary dizionario **m**
die morire
diesel nafta **f**
diet dieta **f**
difference differenza **f**
different diverso/a
difficult difficile
dinghy canotto pneumatico
dining room la sala da pranzo
dinner cena **f**
direct diretto/a
direction direzione **f**
directory (phone) guida telefonica
dirty sporco/a
disabled invalido/a
disappear scomparire
disappointed deluso/a
disaster disastro **m**
disconnected staccato/a
discount sconto **m**
discover scoprire
disease malattia **f**
dish piatto **m**
dishtowel strofinaccio **m**
dishwasher rondella **f**
disinfectant disinfettante **m**
disk disco **m**
disposable diapers/ nappies pannolini usa e getta
distance distanza **f**
district regione **f**

ENGLISH → ITALIAN

disturb disturbare
dive (vb) tuffarsi
diving board trampolino **m**
divorced divorziato/a
DIY shop negozio di bricolage
dizzy vertiginoso/a
do fare
doctor dottore **m**
document documento **m**
dog cane **m**
doll bambola **f**
domestic domestico/a
door porta **f**
doorbell campanello della porta
doorman portiere **m**
double doppio/a
double bed letto matrimoniale
double room camera doppia
doughnut bombolone
downhill in discesa
downstairs al piano di sotto
dozen dozzina **f**
drain tubo di scarico
draught corrente d'aria
draught beer birra alla spina
drawer cassetto **m**
drawing disegno **m**
dreadful terribile
dress vestito **m**
dressing (bandage) fasciatura **f**
dressing (salad) condimento **m**
dressing gown vestaglia **f**
dressing room camerino **m**
drill (n) trapano **m**
drink (n) bevanda **f**
drink (vb) bere
drinking water acqua potabile
drive guidare
driver autista **f**
driving licence patente di guida
drop (n) goccia **f**
drug (med) droga **f**
drug (narcotic) narcotico **m**
drunk ubriaco/a
dry asciutto/a
dry cleaner's tintoria
dryer asciugatore
duck anatra **f**
due dovuto
dull cupo/a
dummy succhiotto **m**
during durante
dust polvere **f**
dustbin pattumiera **f**
duster strofinaccio **m**
dustpan paletta per la spazzatura
Dutch olandese
duty-free esente da dogana

duvet piumone **m**
duvet cover fodera
dye tintura **f**
dynamo dinamo **f**

E

each ogni
eagle aquila **f**
ear orecchio **m**
earache mal d'orecchi
earphones cuffia
earrings orecchini
earth terra **f**
earthquake terremoto **m**
east est
Easter, Happy Easter! Pasqua, Buona Pasqua!
Easter egg uovo di Pasqua
easy facile
eat mangiare
EC CE **f**
economy economia **f**
economy class classe economia
edge bordo **m**
eel anguilla **f**
egg uovo **m**
either of them l'uno o l'altro
elastic elastico/a
elbow gomito **m**
electric elettrico/a
electrician elettricista
electricity elettricità **f**
elevator ascensore **m**
embassy ambasciata **f**
emergency emergenza **f**
emergency exit uscita di sicurezza
empty vuoto/a
end (n) fine **f**
end (vb) finire
engaged (busy) occupato/a
engaged (to be married) fidanzato/a
engine motore **m**
engineer ingegnere **m**
England Inghilterra
English inglese
Englishman/woman inglese **m/f**
enjoy divertirsi
enlargement ingrandimento **m**
enough abbastanza **f**
enquiry domanda **f**
enquiry desk ufficio informazioni
enter entrare
entrance entrata **f**
entrance fee quota d'entrata
envelope busta **f**
epileptic (adj, n) epilettico/a **m/f**
equipment attrezzatura **f**
error errore **m**
escalator scala mobile
escape (n) fuga **f**
escape (vb) sfuggire

especially particolarmente
essential essenziale
estate agent agente immobiliare
Estonia Estonia
EU UE **f**
Europe Europa **f**
European (adj, n) europeo/a **m/f**
even uguale
evening sera **f**
eventually finalmente
every, everyone ogni, ognuno
everything tutto
everywhere dappertutto
exactly esattamente
examination esame **m**
example, for example esempio **m,** per esempio
excellent eccellente
except eccetto
excess luggage bagaglio in eccedenza
exchange scambiare
exciting eccitante
exclude escludere
excursion escursione **f**
excuse me scusi
exhaust pipe tubo di scappamento **m**
exhausted esausto/a
exhibition mostra **f**
exit uscita **f**
expect aspettare, aspettarsi
expenses spese **fpl**
expensive caro/a
experienced esperto/a
expire scadere
explain spiegare
explosion esplosione **f**
export esportare
exposure esposizione **f**
express espresso/a
extension prolungamento **m**
extension lead prolunga
extra più
extraordinary straordinario/a
eye occhio **m**
eye drops goccie per gli occhi
eye make-up remover detergente per trucco
eye shadow ombretto **m**
eyeglasses occhiali **m**

F

face faccia **f**
factory fabbrica **f**
faint (vb) svenire
fair (fête) fiera **f**
fair (hair colour) biondo/a
fair (just) giusto/a
fairly con giustizia, in modo imparziale

fake (adj) falso/a
fake (n) imitazione **f**
fall cadere
false falso/a
family famiglia **f**
famous famoso/a
fan ventilatore **m**
fan belt cinghia del ventilatore
far lontano/a
fare tariffa **f**
farm fattoria **f**
farmer agricoltore **m**
farmhouse casa colonica
fashionable di moda
fast veloce
fasten allacciare
fasten seatbelt allacciare la cintura di sicurezza
fat grasso/a
father padre **m**
father-in-law suocero **m**
fatty grasso/a, grassoccio/a
fault difetto **m**
faulty difettoso/a
favourite preferito/a
fax fax
February febbraio **m**
feed (vb) nutrire
feel sentire
feet piedi **mpl**
female femmina **f**
fence recinto **m**
fender parafango **m**
ferry traghetto **m**
festival festa **f,** festival **m**
fetch andare/venire a prendere
fever febbre f
few, a few pochi, alcuni
fiancé, fiancée fidanzato/a **m/f**
field campo **m**
fight (n) lotta **f**
fight (vb) lottare
file (folder) filza **f**
file (tool) lima **f**
fill riempire
fill in compilare
fill up riempirsi
fillet filetto **m**
filling (tooth) piombatura
film film **m**, pellicola **f**
film processing sviluppare
filter filtro **m**
filthy sudicio/a
find trovare
fine (n) multa **f**
finger dito **m**
finish (vb) finire
fire fuoco **m**
fire brigade vigili del fuoco
fire exit uscita di sicurezza
fire extinguisher estintore **m**

first, at first primo/a, all'inizio
first aid pronto soccorso **m**
first-aid kit cassetta di pronto soccorso
first class di prim' ordine, prima classe
first floor primo piano
first name nome di battesimo
fish pesce **m**
fishing permit permesso di pesca
fishing rod canna da pesca
fishmonger's pescivendolo **m**
fit in buona salute
fitting room sala di prova **f**
fix aggiustare
fizzy frizzante
flag bandiera **f**
flannel flanella **f**
flash lampo **m**
flashlight pila **f**
flask fiasco **m**
flat (n) appartamento **m**
flat battery batteria scarica
flat tyre gomma a terra
flavour sapore **m**
flaw difetto **m**
flea pulce **f**
flight volo **m**
flip flops gli infradito
flippers pinne **f**
flood alluvione **f**
floor pavimento **m**
floorcloth straccio per pavimento
florist fioraio **m**
flour farina **f**
flower fiore **m**
flu influenza **f**
fluent scorrevole, fluente, fluido
fly (n) mosca **f**
fly (vb) volare
fog nebbia **f**
folk gente **f**
follow seguire
food cibo **m**
food poisoning intossicazione alimentare
food shop drogheria **f**
foot piede **m**
football calcio **m**
football match partita di calcio
footpath sentiero **m**
for per
forbidden proibito
forehead fronte **f**
foreign straniero/a
foreigner straniero **m**, forestiero **m**
forest foresta **f**
forget dimenticare
fork forchetta **f**
form modulo **m**
formal formale
fortnight quindicina **f**

fortress fortezza **f**
fortunately fortunatamente
fountain fontana **f**
four-wheel-drive vehicle fuoristrada **f,** veicolo a trazione a 4 ruote
fox volpe **f**
fracture frattura **f**
frame cornice **f**
France Francia **f**
free libero/a
freelance indipendente
freeway autostrada **f**
freezer congelatore **m**
French francese
French fries patatine fritte
Frenchman/woman francese **m/f**
frequent frequente
fresh fresco/a
Friday venerdì
fridge frigo **m**
fried fritto
friend amico/a **m/f**
friendly amichevole
frog rana **f**
from da
front anteriore
frost gelo **m**
frozen congelato
fruit frutta **f**
fruit juice succo di frutta
fruit mince miscuglio di frutta candita
fry friggere
frying pan padella **f**
fuel carburante
fuel gauge indicatore della benzina
full pieno/a
full board pensione completa
fun divertimento **m**
funeral funerale **m**
funicular funicolare **f**
funny divertente
fur pelo **m**
fur coat pelliccia **f**
furnished stanza ammobiliata
furniture mobili **mpl**
further ulteriore
fuse fusibile **m**
fuse box scatola dei fusibili
future futuro **m**

G

gallery galleria **f**
gallon gallone **m**
game gioco **m**
garage garage **m**
garden giardino **m**
garlic aglio **m**
gas benzina **f**
gas cylinder cilindro a gas
gas cooker cucina a gas
gate cancello **m**
gay omosessuale

gay bar bar omosessuale
gear marcia **f**
gear lever leva del cambio
gearbox cambio di velocità
general (adj) generale
generous generoso/a
Geneva Ginevra **f**
gents' toilet toilette per uomini
genuine genuino/a
German (adj, n) tedesco/a **m/f**
German measles rosolia **f**
get ricevere
get off scendere
get on salire
get up alzarsi
gift regalo **m**
girl ragazza **f**
girlfriend amica **f**, ragazza **f**
give dare
give back restituire
glacier ghiacciaio **m**
glad contento/a
glass bicchiere **m**
glasses (spectacles) occhiali
gloves guanti **m**
glue colla **f**
go andare
go away andarsene
go back ritornare
goat capra **f**
God Dio **m**
goggles occhiali di protezione
gold oro **m**
golf club (place) circolo **m** del golf
golf club (stick) mazza da golf
golf course campo di golf
good buono/a
good afternoon, good day buon giorno
good evening buona sera
Good Friday Venerdì Santo
Good luck! Buona fortuna!
good morning buon giorno
good night buonanotte
goodbye arrivederci
goose oca **f**
gothic gotico/a
government governo **m**
gradually gradualmente
gram grammo **m**
grammar grammatica **f**
grand grandioso/a
granddaughter, grandson nipote **m/f**
grandfather nonno **m**
grandmother nonna **f**
grandparents nonni
grape uva
grass erba **f**

grate (vb) grattugiare
grateful grato/a
gravy sugo di carne
greasy untuoso/a, grasso/a, oleoso/a
great grande
Great Britain Gran Bretagna **f**
Greece Grecia **f**
Greek (adj, n) greco **m**
green verde
greengrocer fruttivendolo **m**
greeting saluto **m**
grey grigio/a
grilled alla griglia
ground terra **f,** suolo **m**
ground floor pianterreno **m**
group gruppo **m**
guarantee garanzia **f**
guard guardia **f**
guest ospite **m/f**
guesthouse pensione **f**
guide (n) guida **f**
guide book guida turistica
guided tour escursione con guida
guitar chitarra **f**
gun pistola **f**
gym palestra **f**

H

hail grandine **f**
hair capelli **m**
hairbrush spazzola per capelli
haircut taglio di capelli
hairdresser parrucchiere/a **m/f**
hairdryer asciugacapelli
half metà **f**
hall sala **f**
ham prosciutto **m**
hamburger hamburger
hammer martello **m**
hand mano **f**
hand luggage bagaglio a mano
handbag borsa **f**
handbrake freno a mano
handicapped handicappato/a
handkerchief fazzoletto **m**
handle maniglia **f**
handmade fatto a mano
handsome bello
hang-gliding fare deltaplano **m**
hang up (telephone) riagganciare
hanger attaccapanni
hangover postumi di una sbornia
happen succedere
happy felice
Happy New Year! Buon Anno Nuovo!
harbour porto **m**
hard duro/a
hard disk disco rigido
hardly appena

hardware shop negozio di ferramenta **f**
hare lepre **f**
harvest raccolta **f**
hat cappello **m**
have avere
hay fever raffreddore da fieno
hazelnuts nocciole **f**
he lui
head testa **f,** capo **m**
headache mal di testa
headlights fari **mpl**
headphones cuffie **fpl**
health food shop negozio di macrobiotica
healthy sano/a, in buona salute
hear sentire
hearing aid apparecchio acustico
heart cuore **m**
heart attack infarto
heartburn pirosi
heat calore **m**
heater termosifone, stufa
heating riscaldamento
heavy pesante
heel (foot) tallone **m**
heel (shoe) tacco **m**
height altezza **f**
helicopter elicottero **m**
helmet casco **m**
Help! Aiuto!
help (vb) aiutare
hem orlo **m**
her lei
herbal tea tisana **f**
herbs erbe **f**
here qui, qua
hernia ernia **f**
hide nascondere
high alto/a
high blood pressure pressione alta del sangue
high chair seggiolone **m**
high tide alta marea
him lui
hip fianco **m**
hip replacement sostituto di fianco
hire affittare
hire car macchina a noleggio
his il suo
historic storico/a
history storia **f**
hit colpo **m**
hitchhike fare l'autostop
hold (vb) tenere
hole buco **m**
holiday vacanza **f**
holidays vacanze
holy santo/a
home casa **f**
homesickness nostalgia di casa
honest onesto/a
honey miele **m**
honeymoon luna di miele
hood (of car) cofano **m**
hood (of garment) cappuccio **m**

hope (n) speranza **f**
hope (vb) sperare
hopefully con speranza
horn (animal) corno **m**
horn (car) tromba **f**, clacson **m**
horse cavallo **m**
horse racing corse di cavalli
horse riding equitazione (del cavallo)
hose pipe tubo flessibile
hospital ospedale **m**
hospitality ospitalità **f**
hostel ostello **m**
hot caldo/a
hot spring sorgente calda
hot-water bottle borsa per acqua calda
hour ora **f**
hourly ogni ora
house casa **f**
house wine vino di casa
housework lavoro domestico
hovercraft hovercraft **m**
How? Come?
How are you? Come stai ?
How do you do? Molto lieto!
How many? Quanti?
How much do I owe you? Quanto le devo?
How much is it? Quanto costa questo?
humid umido/a
humour umorismo **m**
Hungarian (adj, n) ungherese **m/f**
Hungary Ungheria **f**
hungry: I am hungry ho fame
hunt (n) caccia **f**
hunt (vb) cacciare
hunting permit permesso per caccia
hurry (n) fretta **f**
hurry (vb) affrettare
hurt, it hurts far male, mi fa male
husband marito **m**
hydrofoil aliscafo **m**
hypodermic needle ago ipodermico

I

I io
ice ghiaccio **m**
ice cream gelato **m**
ice rink pista di pattinaggio
ice skates pattini da ghiaccio
iced coffee caffè ghiacciato
idea idea **f**
identity card carta d'identità
if se
ignition accensione **f**
ignition key chiave dell'accensione
ill malato/a
illness malattia **f**

ENGLISH → ITALIAN

immediately immediatamente
important importante
impossible impossibile
improve migliorare
in in, nel
inch pollice **m**
included incluso
inconvenient scomodo/a
incredible incredibile
Indian (adj, n) indiano/a **m/f**
indicator freccia **f**
indigestion indigestione **f**
indoor pool piscina coperta, piscina interna
indoors dentro
infection infenzione **f**
infectious infettivo/a
inflammation infiammazione **f**
informal informale
information informazioni **f**
ingredients ingredienti **mpl**
injection iniezione **f**
injured ferito/a
injury ferita **f**
ink inchiostro **m**
in-laws parenti acquisiti
inn locanda **f**
inner tube camera d'aria **f**
insect insetto **m**
insect bite puntura di insetto **m**
insect repellent insettifugo **m**
inside interno
insist insistere
insomnia insonnia **f**
instant coffee caffè solubile
instead invece
insulin insulina **f**
insurance assicurazione **f**
intelligent intelligente
interesting interessante
international internazionale
interpreter interprete **m/f**
intersection intersezione **f**
interval intervallo **m**
into dentro a
introduce presentare
invitation invito **m**
invite invitare
invoice fattura **f**
Ireland Irlanda **f**
Irish irlandese
Irishman/woman irlandese **m/f**
iron ferro da stiro
ironing board asse da stiro
ironmonger's negozio di ferramenta
is è
island isola **f**

it lo **m**, la **f**
Italian (adj, n) italiano/a **m/f**
Italy Italia **f**
itch (n) prurito **m**

J

jack cricco **m**
jacket giacca **f**
jam marmellata **f**
jammed congestionato
janitor portinaio/a **m/f**
January gennaio **m**
jar barattolo **m**
jaundice itterizia **f**
jaw mascella **f**
jealous geloso/a
jellyfish medusa **f**
jersey maglia **f**
Jew ebreo **m**
jeweller's gioielleria **f**
jewellery gioielli **m**
Jewish ebraico/a
job lavoro **m**
jog fare jogging
join unire
joint giuntura **f**
joke scherzo **m**
journey viaggio **m**
joy gioia **f**
jug brocca **f**
judge (n) giudice
judge (vb) giudicare
juice succo **m**
July luglio **m**
jump saltare
jump leads cavi con morsetti
jumper golf **m**
junction giunzione **m**, congiungimento **m**, raccordo **m**
June giugno **m**
just (fair) giusto/a
just (only) proprio, appena

K

keep tenere
Keep the change! Tenga il resto!
kettle bollitore (per l'acqua)
key chiave **f**
key ring portachiavi **m**
kick (n) calcio **m**
kick (vb) prendere a calci
kidney rene **m**
kill uccidere
kilo, kilogram chilo **m**, chilogrammo **m**
kilometre chilometro **m**
kind (adj) gentile
kind (n) sorta **f**
king re **m**
kiosk chiosco **m**
kiss (n) bacio **m**
kiss (vb) baciare
kitchen cucina **f**
kitchenette cucinino **m**
knee ginocchio **m**
knickers mutandine **f**
knife coltello **m**
knit lavorare a maglia
knit wear maglieria **f**

knitting needle ferro da calza
knock bussare
knock down investire
knock over rovesciare
know sapere

L

label etichetta **f**
lace (fabric) pizzo **m**
lace (for shoe) laccio **m**
ladder scala **f**
ladies' toilet toilette per donne
ladies' wear l'abbigliamento da donna
lady signora **f**
lager birra **f**
lake lago **m**
Lake Garda Lago di Garda
Lake Maggiore Lago Maggiore
lamb agnello **m**
lamp lampada **f**
land terra **f**
landlady proprietaria **f**
landlord proprietario **m**
landslide frana **f**
lane sentiero **m**
language lingua **f**
language course corso di lingua
large grande
last ultimo/a
last night ieri sera, ieri notte
last week scorsa settimana
late ritardo/a, tardi
later più tardi
Latvia Lettonia **f**
laugh (n) risata **f**
laugh (vb) ridere
launderette, laundromat lavanderia **f**
laundry bucato **m**
lavatory gabinetto **m**
law legge **f**
lawyer avvocato **m**
laxative lassativo **m**
lazy pigro/a
lead (n) piombo **m**
lead (vb) condurre
lead-free senza piombo
leaf foglia **f**
leaflet volantino **m**
leak (n) perdita **f**
leak (vb) perdere
learn imparare
lease (n) contratto d'affitto **m**
lease (vb) affittare
leather pelle **f**
leave lasciare
leek porro **m**
left sinistra
left-handed mancino/a
leg gamba **f**
lemon limone **m**
lemonade limonata **f**
lend prestare

lens lente **f**
lentils lenticchie **f**
lesbian lesbica **f**
less meno
lesson lezione **f**
let (allow) permettere
let off (oneself) lasciarsi andare
letter lettera **f**
letterbox buca per le lettere
lettuce lattuga **f**
level crossing passaggio a livello
lever leva **f**
library biblioteca **f**
licence licenza **f**, patente **f** (for driving)
lid coperchio **m**
lie (n, untruth) bugia **f**
lie (vb, fib) mentire
lie (vb, recline) giacere
lie down sdraiarsi
life vita **f**
life belt salvagente **m**
life guard bagnino **m**
life insurance assicurazione sulla vita
life jacket giubbotto di salvataggio
lift (n, elevator) ascensore **m**
lift (vb) sollevare
light (adj, not dark) chiaro/a
light (adj, not heavy) leggero/a
light (n) luce **f**
light bulb lampadina **f**
lightning lampo **m**
like (adj) simile
like (prep) come, da
like (vb) piacere
lime calce **f**
linen lino **m**
lingerie biancheria **f**
lion leone **m**
lipstick rossetto **m**
liqueur liquore
list lista **f**
listen ascoltare
Lithuania Lituania **f**
litre litro **m**
litter (n) rifiuti **mpl**
litter (vb) disseminare
little piccolo/a, poco/a
live vivere
lively vivace
liver fegato **m**
living room soggiorno **m**
loaf pagnotta **f**
lobby atrio **m**
lobster aragosta **f**
local locale
lock (n) serratura **f**
lock (vb) chiudere
lock in chiudere dentro
lock out chiudere fuori
locker armadietto **m**
lollipop lecca-lecca
long (adj) lungo/a
long (adv) lungamente
long-distance call chiamata interurbana
look after badare

look at guardare
look for cercare
look forward to essere impaziente di
loose libero/a
lorry camion **m**
lose perdere
lost perduto/a
lost property oggetti smarriti
lot molto
loud forte
lounge salotto **m**
love (n) amore **m**
love (vb) amare
lovely bello/a
low basso/a
low fat magro
low tide bassa marea
luck fortuna **f**
lucky fortunato/a
luggage bagaglio **m**
luggage rack portabagagli **m**
luggage tag etichetta per bagagli
luggage trolley carello portabagagli
lump bernoccolo **m**
lunch pranzo **m**
lung polmone **m**
Luxembourg Lussenburgo
luxury lusso **m**

M
machine macchina **f**
mad pazzo/a
made fatto/a
magazine rivista **f**
maggot verme **m**
magnet magnete **m**
magnifying glass lente d'ingrandimento
maid cameriera **f**
maiden name cognome da nubile
mail (n) posta **f**
mail (vb) impostare
main principale
main course portata principale
main post office l'ufficio postale principale
main road strada principale
mains switch interruttore principale
make fare
male maschile
man uomo **m**
man-made fibre tessuto sintetico
manager direttore **m**
manual (adj) manuale
manual (n) manuale **m**
many molti
map carta geografica **f**
marble (n, stone) marmo **m**
marble (n, toy) pallina **f**
March marzo m
market mercato **m**

marmalade marmellata d'arance
married sposato/a
marsh palude **f**
mascara mascara **m**
mashed potatoes purè di patate
mass (volume) massa **f**
Mass (rel) Messa **f**
mast albero **m**
match (n, game) incontro **m**
matches (for lighting) fiammiferi **mpl**
material stoffa **f**
matter faccenda **f**
matter: It doesn't matter Non importa
matter: What's the matter? Che cosa c'è?
mattress materasso **m**
May maggio **m**
may (vb, be able to) potere
maybe forse
mayonnaise maionese **f**
me mi
meal pasto **m**
mean (adj, nasty) meschino/a
mean (vb, intend) intendere
measles morbillo **m**
measure (n) misura **f**
measure (vb) misurare
meat carne **f**
mechanic meccanico **m**
medical insurance assicurazione sanitaria
medicine medicina **f**
medieval medievale
Mediterranean mediterraneo
medium medio/a
medium dry (wine) vino amabile
medium rare (meat) non troppo cotto/a
medium sized di taglia media
meet incontrare
meeting incontro **m**
melon melone **m**
melt sciogliere
men uomini **m**
mend riparare
meningitis meningite **f**
menswear l'abbigliamento da uomo
mention (n) menzione **f**
mention (vb) menzionare
menu menu **m**
meringue meringa **f**
message messaggio **m**
metal metallo **m**
meter contatore **m**
metre metro **m**
metro la metropolitana
microwave forno a microonde
midday mezzogiorno **m**
middle di mezzo **m**

ENGLISH → ITALIAN

ENGLISH → ITALIAN

midnight mezzanotte
might potere
migraine emicrania **f**
mile miglio **m**
milk latte **m**
mind (n) mente **f**, intelligenza **f**
mind (vb, take care) badare
mineral water acqua minerale
minister (church) pastore **m**
minister (politics) ministro **m**
mint menta **f**
minute (adj, size) minuto/a
minute (n, time) minuto **m**
mirror specchio **m**
Miss signorina
miss (vb) mancare
missing mancante
mist foschia **f**
mistake sbaglio **m**
misunderstanding malinteso **m**
mix mescolare
mix up confondere
mobile phone telefono cellulare
moisturizer crema idratante
moment momento **m**
monastery monastero **m**
Monday lunedì **m**
money soldi **m**
money belt cintura portasoldi
money order vaglia postale
month mese **m**
monthly mensile
monument monumento **m**
moon luna **f**
mooring ormeggio **m**
more più
morning mattina **f**
mosque moschea **f**
mosquito zanzara **f**
most la maggior parte di
mostly per lo più
moth falena **f**
mother madre **f**
mother-in-law suocera **f**
motor motore **m**
motorbike motocicletta **f**
motorboat motoscafo **m**
motorway autostrada **f**
mountain montagna **f**
mountain rescue soccorso alpino
mountaineering alpinismo **m**
mouse topo **m**
moustache baffi **m**
mouth bocca **f**
mouth ulcer stomatite
mouthwash colluttorio **m**, acqua dentifricia **f**

move muovere
Mr Signor **m**
Mrs/Ms Signora **f**, Signorina **f**
much molto/a
mud fango **m**
mug boccale **m**
mugged aggredito/a e derubato/a
mumps orecchioni **mpl**
Munich Monaco di Baviera
muscle muscolo **m**
museum museo **m**
mushroom fungo **m**
musician musicista **m/f**
Muslim musulmano **m**
mussels cozze **fpl**
must dovere
mustard senape **f**
mutton carne di montone
my il mio **m**, la mia **f**
myself io stesso

N
nail unghia **f**
nail brush spazzolino da unghie **m**
nail file limetta da unghie **f**
nail polish/varnish smalto per unghie **m**
nail polish remover acetone
nail scissors forbicine da unghie
name nome **m**
nanny bambinaia **f**
napkin tovagliolo **m**
nappy pannolino **m**
narrow stretto/a
nasty cattivo/a
national nazionale
nationality nazionalità **f**
natural naturale
nature natura **f**
nature reserve riserva naturale **f**
nausea nausea **f**
navy marina **f**
navy blue blu marino **m**
near vicino
nearby vicino
nearly quasi
necessary necessario/a
neck collo **m**
necklace collana **f**
need (n) bisogno **m**
need (vb) bisognare
needle ago **m**
negative negativo/a
neighbour vicino/a **m/f**
neither ... nor nè ... nè
nephew nipote **m**
nest nido **m**
net rete **f**
Netherlands Paesi Bassi
never mai
new nuovo/a
New Year Anno Nuovo
New Year's Eve Vigilia di Capodanno
New Zealand Nuova Zelanda **f**

ENGLISH → ITALIAN

New Zealander Neozelandese **m/f**
news notizie **fpl**
news stand edicola **f**
newspaper giornale **m**
next prossimo/a
next week la prossima settimana
nice bello/a
niece nipote **f**
night notte **f**
nightdress camicia da notte
no no
nobody nessuno **m**
noise rumore **m**
noisy rumoroso/a
non-alcoholic analcolico **m**
non-smoking non fumatori
none niente
noon mezzogiorno
north nord **m**
North Sea Mare del Nord **m**
Northern Ireland Irlanda del Nord **f**
Norway Norvegia **f**
Norwegian norvegese **m/f**
nose naso **m**
not non
note nota **f**
notebook/paper taccuino **m**, carta da lettere
nothing niente, nulla
nothing else nient'altro
notice board tabellone
novel romanzo **m**
November novembre **m**
now adesso
nudist beach spiaggia per nudisti
number numero **m**
number plate targa **f**
nurse, male nurse infermiera, infermiere
nursery stanza dei bambini
nursery school scuola materna **f**
nursery slope pista per principianti
nut noce f
nut (for bolt) dado **m**

O

oak quercia **f**
oar remo **m**
oats avena **f**
obtain ottenere
occasionally ogni tanto
occupation occupazione **f**
occupied (e.g. toilet) occupato/a
ocean oceano **m**
October ottobre **m**
odd (of numbers) dispari
odd (strange) strano/a
of di
off spento
office ufficio **m**

often spesso
oil olio **m**
ointment pomata **f**
okay va bene
old vecchio/a
old-age pensioner pensionato **m**
old-fashioned antiquato/a
olive oliva **f**
olive oil olio di oliva
omelette omelette **f,** frittata **f**
on su, sopra
once una volta **f**
one uno, una
one-way street senso unico
onion cipolla **f**
only solo
open aperto/a
open ticket biglietto aperto **m**
opening times orario d'apertura
opera opera f
operation operazione **f**
operator (phone) centralinista **m/f**
opposite opposto/a
optician ottico **m**
or o
orange arancia **f**
orange juice succo d'arancia
orchestra orchestra **f**
order (n) ordine **m**
order (vb) ordinare
organic (vegetables) organico/a
other altro/a
otherwise altrimenti
our nostro/a
out fuori
out of order guasto
outdoors all'aperto
outside esterno **m**
oven forno **m**
ovenproof pirofilo/ resistente al calore
over sopra
over here qui
over there là
overcharged far pagare più del dovuto
overcoat cappotto **m**
overdone stracotto
overheat surriscaldare
overnight per la notte
overtake sorpassare
owe dovere
owl gufo **m**
owner proprietario/a **m/f**

P

pacemaker pacemaker **m**
pack (of cards) mazzo **m**
package pacco **m**
package holiday vacanza organizzata
packet pacchetto **m**
padlock lucchetto **m**
page pagina **f**
paid pagato

ENGLISH → ITALIAN

ENGLISH → ITALIAN

pail secchio **m**
pain dolore **m**
painful doloroso/a
painkiller analgesico **m**
paint (n) pittura **f**
paint (vb) pitturare
painting (picture) quadro **m**
pair paio **m**
palace palazzo **m**
pale pallido/a
pan padella **f**
pancake frittella **f**
panties mutandine **f**
pants mutande **f**
pantyhose collant **m**
paper carta **f**
paper napkins tovaglioli di carta
parcel pacco **m**
Pardon? Scusi?
parents genitori **m**
parents-in-law suoceri **m**
park (n) parco **m**
park (vb) parcheggiare
parking disc disco parcheggio **m**
parking meter parchimetro **m**
parking ticket multa per divieto di sosta
part parte **f**
partner (business) socio **m**
partner (companion) compagno/a **m/f**
party (celebration) festa **f**
party (political) partito **m**
pass (n) passo **m**
pass (vb) passare
pass control controllo **m**
passenger passeggero **m**
passport passaporto **m**
past passato/a
pastry pasta **f**
path sentiero **m**
patient (adj) paziente
patient (n) paziente **m/f**
pattern disegno **m**
pavement marciapiede **m**
pay pagare
payment pagamento **m**
payphone telefono pubblico **m**
pea pisello **m**
peach pesca **f**
peak picco **m**
peak rate tariffa massima **f**
peanut arachide **m**
pear pera **f**
pearl perla **f**
peculiar strano/a
pedal pedale **m**
pedestrian pedone **m**
pedestrian crossing passaggio pedonale

peel (n) buccia **f**
peel (vb) sbucciare
peg piolo **m**
pen penna **f**
pencil matita **f**
penfriend amico di penna
peninsula penisola **f**
pensioner pensionato **m**
people persone **f**
pepper pepe **m**
per per
perfect perfetto/a
performance esecuzione **f**
perfume profumo **m**
perhaps forse
period periodo **m**
perm permanente
permit (n) permesso **m**
permit (vb) permettere
person persona **f**
pet animale domestico **m**
petrol benzina **f**
petrol can latta per benzina **f**
petrol station stazione di servizio
pharmacy farmacia **f**
phone telefono **m**
phone book elenco telefonico **m**
phone booth cabina telefonica **f**
phone call telefonata **f**
phone card scheda telefonica **f**
phone number numero telefonico **m**
photo, to take a photo foto f, fare una foto
photocopy fotocopia **f**
phrase book libro di fraseologia
piano piano **m**
pickpocket borsaiolo **m**
picnic picnic **m**
picture disegno **m**
picture frame cornice **f**
pie torta **f**
piece pezzo **m**
pig maiale **m**
pill pillola **f**
pillow guanciale **m**
pillowcase federa **f**
pilot pilota **f**
pin spillo **m**
pineapple ananas **m**
pink rosa
pipe pipa **f**
pity, It's a pity peccato, È un peccato
place (n) posto **m**
place (vb) posare, porre
plain semplice
plait treccia **f**
plane aeroplano **m**
plant (n) pianta **f**
plant (vb) piantare
plaster gesso **m**
plastic plastica **f**

ENGLISH → ITALIAN

plastic bag sacchetto di plastica
plate piatto **m**
platform binario **m**
play (n, game) gioco **m**
play (n, theatre) dramma **m**
play (vb) giocare
playground cortile **m**
please per favore
pleased lieto/a
Pleased to meet you! Molto lieto/piacere!
plenty abbondanza **f**
pliers pinze **f**
plug (bath) tappo **m**
plug (elec) spina **f**
plum prugna **f**
plumber idraulico **m**
p.m. (after noon) del pomeriggio
poached egg uovo in camicia
pocket tasca **f**
point (n) punto **m**
point (vb) indicare
points (car) puntine **f**
poison veleno **m**
poisonous velenoso/a
Poland Polonia f
police polizia f
police station commissariato **m**
policeman poliziotto **m**
policewoman (donna) poliziotta
Polish polacco **m**
polish (n) lucido **m**
polish (vb) lucidare
polite cortese
polluted inquinato
pool pozza **f**
poor (impoverished) povero/a
poor (quality) scandente
poppy papavero **m**
popular popolare
population popolazione
pork carne di maiale
port (harbour) porto **m**
port (wine) Vino di Oporto **m**
porter portiere **m**
portion porzione **f**
portrait ritratto **m**
Portugal Portogallo **m**
Portuguese (adj, n) portoghese **m/f**
posh danaroso/a
possible possibile
post (n) posta **f**
post (vb) impostare
post box cassetta delle lettere
post office ufficio postale
postage affrancatura **f**
postage stamp francobollo **m**
postal code codice postale
postcard cartolina **f**
poster manifesto **m**

postman/woman postino/a **m/f**
postpone rimandare
potato patata **f**
pothole buca **f**
pottery ceramica **f**
pound (money) sterlina **f**
pound (weight) libbra **f**
pour versare
powder polvere **f**
powdered milk latte in polvere
power cut interruzione di corrente
practice pratica **f**
practise praticare
pram carrozzella **f**
prawn gambero **m**
pray pregare
prefer preferire
pregnant incinta
prescription ricetta **f**
present (adj) presente
present (n) regalo **m**
present (vb) presentare
pressure pressione **f**
pretty carino/a
price prezzo **m**
priest prete **m**
Prime Minister Primo Ministro **m**
print (n) stampa **f**
print (vb) stampare
printed matter stampe
prison prigione **f**
private privato/a
prize premio m
probably probabilmente
problem problema **m**
programme, program programma **m**
prohibited vietato
promise promessa **f**
pronounce pronunciare
properly correttamente
Protestant protestante
public pubblico/a
public holiday festa nazionale
pudding dolce **m**
pull tirare
pullover maglione **m**
pump (n) pompa **f**
pump (vb) pompare
puncture foratura **f**
puppet show spettacolo burattini **m**
purple viola
purse borsellino **m**
push spingere
pushchair passeggino **m**
put mettere
put up (guest) ospitare
pyjamas pigiama **f**

Q

quality qualità **f**
quantity quantità **f**
quarantine quarantena **f**
quarrel (n) lite **f**
quarrel (vb) litigare

ENGLISH → ITALIAN

quarter quarto **m**
quay banchina **f**
queen regina **f**
question (n) domanda **f**
question (vb) domandare
queue fila **f**
quickly fretta, presto
quiet tranquillo/a
quilt trapunta **f**
quite completamente

R
rabbit coniglio **m**
rabies rabbia **f**
race (people) razza **f**
race (sport) corsa **f**
race course ippodromo **m**
racket racchetta **f**
radiator radiatore **m**
radio radio **f**
radish ravanello **m**
rag straccio **m**
railway ferrovia **f**
railway station stazione ferroviaria
rain pioggia **f**
raincoat impermeabile **m**
raisin uva passa
rake rastrello **m**
rape (n) violazione **f**
rape (vb) violentare
rare raro/a
rash eruzione **f**
raspberry lampone **m**
rat topo m
rate (of exchange) tasso **m**
raw crudo/a
razor rasoio **m**
razor blades lamette da barba
read leggere
ready pronto
real vero/a
realize realizzare
really davvero
rear-view mirror specchietto retrovisore
reasonable ragionevole
receipt ricevuta **f**
receiver ricevitore **m**
recently recentemente
reception ricezione **f**
receptionist impiegato ricezione
recharge ricaricare
recipe ricetta **f**
recognize riconoscere
recommend raccomandare
record (n) documento **m**
record (vb) registrare
red rosso
red wine vino rosso **m**
redcurrants mirtilli rossi
reduce ridurre
reduction riduzione **f**
refund (n) rimborso **m**
refund (vb) rimborsare
refuse (n) immondizia **f**
refuse (vb) rifiutare

region regione **f**
register (n) registro **m**
register (vb) registrare
registered mail posta raccomandata
registration form modulo registrazione
registration number targa **f**
relative, relation parente **m/f**
remain restare
remember ricordare
rent (n) affitto **m**
rent (vb) affittare
repair (n) riparazione **f**
repair (vb) riparare
repeat ripetere
reply (n) risposta **f**
reply (vb) rispondere
report (n) rapporto **m**
report (vb) rapportare
request (n) richiesta **f**
request (vb) richiedere
require richiedere
rescue (n) salvamento **m**
rescue (vb) salvare
reservation (seats) prenotazione **f**
reserve riserva **f**
resident residente **m/f**
resort luogo di villeggiatura
rest (n, relaxation) riposo **m**
rest (n, remainder) resto **m**
rest (vb) riposare
retired andare in pensione
return (n) ritorno **m**
return (vb) ritornare
return ticket biglietto di andata e ritorno
reverse invertire
reverse-charge call chiamata a carico del destinatario
reverse gear marcia indietro
revolting rivoltante
rheumatism reumatismo **m**
rib costola **f**
ribbon nastro **m**
rice riso **m**
rich ricco/a
ridiculous ridicolo/a
ride (n) cavalcata **f**
ride (vb) cavalcare
right (correct) corretto/a
right (direction) destro/a
right (fair) giusto/a
right-hand drive guida a destra
ring (n) anello **m**
ring (vb) suonare
ring road circonvallazione **f**
ripe maturo/a
rip-off frode **f**
river fiume **m**
road strada **f**

road accident incidente
road map carta stradale **f**
road sign cartello/ segnale stradale **m**
roadworks lavori stradali **m**
rock roccia **f**
roll panino **m**
roof tetto **m**
roof-rack portabagagli **m**
room camera **f**
rope corda **f**
rose rosa **f**
rotten marcio/a
rough ruvido/a
roughly pressappoco
round rotondo/a
roundabout giostra **f**
row (n, queue) fila **f**
row (n, noise) rumore **m**
row (vb, boat) remare
royal reale
rubber gomma **f**
rubbish immondizia **f**
rubella rosolia **f**
rudder timone **m**
rug tappeto **m**
ruin (n) rovina **f**
ruin (vb) rovinare
ruler (for measuring) regolo **m**
ruler (sovereign) sovrano **m**
rum rum **m**
run correre
rush (n) fretta **f**
rush (vb) affrettare
rusty arrugginito/a
rye bread pane di segale **f**

S

sad triste
saddle sella **f**
safe sicuro/a
safety belt cintura di sicurezza
safety pin spillo di sicurezza **m**
sail (n) vela **f**
sail (vb) navigare
sailing navigazione **f**
salad insalata **f**
salad dressing condimento per insalata
sale vendita **f**
sales representative rappresentante **m**
salesperson venditore **m**
salmon salmone **m**
salt sale **m**
same stesso/a
sand sabbia **f**
sandals sandali **mpl**
sandwich tramezzino **m**
sanitary pads assorbenti igienici **m**
Saturday sabato
sauce salsa **f**
saucer piattino **m**
sausage salsiccia **f**

save salvare
savoury salato/a, saporito
say dire
scale bilancia **f**
scarf sciarpa **f**
scenery scenario **m**
school scuola **f**
scissors forbici **f**
Scot scozzese **m/f**
Scotland Scozia **f**
Scottish scozzese
scrambled eggs uova strapazzate
scratch (n) graffio **m**
scratch (vb) graffiare
screen schermo **m**
screw (n) vite **f**
screw (vb) avvitare
screwdriver cacciavite **m**
scrubbing brush spazzolino per le unghie
scuba diving immersioni subacquee
sea mare **m**
seagull gabbiano **m**
seasickness mal di mare
seaside spiaggia **f**
seaweed alga marina **f**
season stagione **f**
season ticket abbonamento **m**
seasoning condimento **m**
seat sedia **f**
seat belt cintura di sicurezza **f**
secluded appartato/a
second (adj, number) secondo/a
second (n, of time) secondo **m**
second class seconda classe
second hand (of clock) lancetta dei secondi **f**
second-hand (used) usato, di seconda
secretary segretario **m**
security guard guardia di sicurezza
see vedere
self-catering in un appartamento attrezza to di cucina
self-employed che lavora in proprio
self-service self service
sell vendere
sell-by date data di scadenza **f**
send mandare
senior citizen anziano **m**
sentence (grammar) frase **f**
sentence (law) sentenza **f**
separate (adj) separato/a
separate (vb) separare

September settembre **m**
septic settico/a
septic tank fossa biologica/settica **f**
serious serio/a
service servizio **m**
service charge servizio **m**
set menu menù fisso
several parecchi
sew cucire
sex (gender) sesso **m**
sex (intercourse) coito **m**
shade ombra **f**
shake scuotere
shallow poco profondo
shame vergogna **f**
shampoo and set shampoo e messa in piega
share (n) parte **f**
share (vb) dividere
sharp tagliente
shave radere
she lei **f**
sheep pecora **f**
sheet lenzuolo **m**
shelf scaffale **m**
shellfish frutti di mare
sheltered ritirato/a
shine splendere
shingle ghiaia **f**
shingles fuochi di Sant'Antonio
ship nave **f**
shirt camicia **f**
shock absorber ammortizzatore **m**
shoe scarpa **f**
shoe laces lacci da scarpa
shop negozio **m**
shop assistant commesso **m**
shop window vetrina **f**
shopping centre centro commerciale **m**
shore riva **f**
short corto/a
short-cut scorciatoia **f**
short-sighted miope
shorts calzoncini corti
should dovere
shoulder spalla **f**
shout (n) grido **m**
shout (vb) gridare
show (n) mostra **f**
show (vb) mostrare
shower doccia **f**
shrimps gamberetti **mpl**
shrink restringersi
shut chiudere
shutter serranda **f**
shy timido/a
sick, I'm going to be sick! ammalato/a, Mi sento male!/Ho voglia di vomitare!
side lato **m**
side dish contorno **m**
sidewalk marciapiede **m**
sieve setaccio **m**
sight vista **f**

sightseeing andare a visitare posti
sign (n) segno **m**
sign (vb) firmare
signal segnale **m**
signature firma **f**
signpost segnale stradale **f**
silence silenzio **m**
silk seta **f**
silly sciocco/a
silver argento **m**
similar simile
simple semplice
sing cantare
singer cantante **m/f**
single solo
single bed letto singolo
single room camera singola
single ticket biglietto di andata
sink lavandino **m**
sister sorella **f**
sister-in-law cognata **f**
sit sedere
size misura **f**
skate (n) pattino **m**
skate (vb) pattinare
skating rink pista di pattinaggio
ski (n) sci **m**
ski (vb) sciare
ski boot scarponi da sci
ski jump trampolino per sci
ski slope pista per sci
skin pelle **f**
skirt gonna **f**
sky cielo **m**
sledge slitta **f**
sleep dormire
sleeping bag sacco a pelo **m**
sleeping car vagone letto
sleeping pill sonnifero **m**
sleepy assonnato/a
slice (n) fetta **f**
slice (vb) affettare
slide (n) scivolo **m**
slide (vb) scivolare
slip (n) scivolata **f**
slip (vb) scivolare
slippers pantofole **f**
slippery scivoloso
slow lento/a
slowly lentamente
small piccolo/a
smell (n) odore **m**
smell (vb) odorare
smile (n) sorriso **m**
smile (vb) sorridere
smoke (n) fumo **m**
smoke (vb) fumare
smoked salmon salmone affumicato
snack spuntino **m**
snake serpente **m**
sneeze (n) starnuto **m**
sneeze (vb) starnutire
snore russare
snorkel respiratore **m**

snow, it is snowing neve **f,** nevica
soaking solution soluzione per lenti a contatto
soap sapone **m**
soap powder detersivo in polvere
sober sobrio/a
socket presa di corrente
socks calzini **m**
soda soda **f**
soft morbido/a
soft drink bibita analcolica **f**
sole (fish) sogliola **f**
sole (foot) pianta **f**
sole (shoe) suola **f**
soluble solubile
some alcuni, qualche
someone, somebody qualcuno **m**
something qualcosa
sometimes qualche volta
somewhere da qualche parte
son figlio **m**
son-in-law genero **m**
song canzone **f**
soon presto
sore, it's sore dolorante, fa male
sore throat mal di gola
Sorry! Mi dispiace!
sort (n) specie **f**
sort (vb) classificare
soup minestra **f**
sour agro/a
south sud **m**
South Africa Sudafrica **f**
South African (adj, n) sudafricano/a **m/f**
souvenir ricordo souvenir **m**
spa stazione termale **f**
spade vanga **f**
Spain Spagna **f**
Spaniard spagnolo/a **m/f**
Spanish spagnoli/e **m/f**
spanner chiave inglese
spare part pezzo di ricambio
spare tyre/wheel ruota di scorta
spark plug candela **f**
sparkling frizzante
speak parlare
speciality specialità
spectacles occhiali **m**
speed velocità **f**
speed limit limite di velocità
speedometer tachimetro **m**
spell (n, magic) incantesimo **m**
spell (vb, grammar) compitare
spend spendere
spice spezia **f**
spider ragno **m**
spill rovesciare
spinach spinaci **m**
spin-dryer centrifuga **f**

spine spina dorsale **f**
spirits spirito **m**
splinter scheggia **f**
spoil rovinare
spoke raggio **m**
sponge spugna **f**
spoon cucchiaio **m**
sprain (vb) slogare
spring (metal) molla **f**
spring (season) primavera **f**
square (adj) quadrato/a
square (n) piazza **f**
stadium stadio **m**
stain macchia **f**
stairs scale **f**
stale stantio/a
stalls bancarelle **f**
stamp francobollo **m**
staple fermare con una graffa
star (film) divo/a **m/f**
star (sky) stella **f**
start cominciare
starter (car) avviatore **m**
starter (meal) antipasto **m**
station stazione **f**
stationer's cartoleria **f**
statue statua **f**
stay rimanere
steal rubare
steam vapore **m**
steep ripido/a
steer sterzare
steering wheel volante
step gradino **m**
stepfather patrigno **m**
stepmother matrigna **f**
stew stufato **m**
stick (n) bastone **m**
stick (vb) aderire
sticking plaster cerotto **m**
still ancora
sting (n) puntura **f**
sting (vb) pungere
stitch punto **m**
stock scorta **f**
stocking calza **f**
stolen rubato
stomach stomaco **m**
stomachache mal di stomaco
stone pietra **f**
stop (n) fermata **f**
stop (vb) fermare
stop over pernottare
store magazzino **m**
storey piano **m**
storm tempesta f
straight diritto/a
straight on tirare diritto
straightaway immediatamente, subito
strange strano/a
stranger estraneo **m**
strap cinghia **f**
straw paglia **f**
strawberry fragola **f**
stream ruscello **m**
street strada **f**
street map pianta stradale

strike sciopero **m**
string corda **f**
striped a strisce
stroke colpo **m**
strong forte
stuck inceppato
student studente **m**
student discount sconto per studenti
stuffed ripieno **m**
stupid stupido/a
subtitle sottotitolo **m**
suburb sobborgo **m**
subway metropolitana **f**
suddenly improvvisamente
suede camoscio **m**
sugar zucchero **m**
sugar-free senza zucchero
suit vestito **m**
suitcase valigia **f**
summer estate **f**
summit cima **f**
sun sole **m**
sun block crema solare
sunburn scottatura **f**
Sunday domenica **f**
sunglasses occhiali da sole
sunny assolato/a
sunrise alba **f**
sunroof tettuccio apribile
sunset tramonto **m**
sunshade parasole **m**
sunshine luce del sole
sunstroke insolazione **f**
suntan oil olio solare
suntanned abbronzato/a
supper cena **f**
supplement supplemento **m**
sure certo/a, sicuro/a
surfboard tavola da surf
surgery (doctor's rooms) gabinetto medico
surgery (procedure) chirurgia **f**
surname cognome **m**
surrounded circondato
suspension sospensione **f**
swallow inghiottire
swear (an oath) giurare
swear (curse) bestemmiare
swear word parolaccia **f**, bestemmia **f**
sweat (n) sudore **m**
sweat (vb) sudare
sweater maglione **m**
Swede svedese **m/f**
Sweden Svezia **f**
Swedish svedese
sweet dolce
swell gonfiare
swelling gonfiore **m**
swim nuotare
swimming costume costume da bagno **m**
swing altalena **f**
Swiss svizzero/a **m/f**

Swiss-German svizzero/a tedesco/a
switch interruttore **m**
switch off spegnere
switch on accendere
Switzerland Svizzera **f**
swollen gonfio/a
synagogue sinagoga **f**

T

table tavolo m
table wine vino da tavola
tablecloth tovaglia **f**
tablespoon cucchiaio (da tavola)
tailor sarto **m**
take prendere
take-away food piatto da portar via, fuori, piatto da asporto
take care badare
talcum powder talco **m**
talk parlare
tall alto/a
tampon tampone **m**
tan abbronzatura **f**
tangerine mandarino **m**
tank serbatoio **m**
tape nastro **m**
tape measure metro **m**
tape recorder registratore **m**
taste (n) gusto **m**
taste (vb) assaggiare
tax tassa **f**
taxi taxi, tassì
taxi driver tassista **m/f**
taxi rank posteggio per taxi
tea tè
teabag bustina di tè
teach insegnare
teacher insegnante **m/f**
team squadra **f**
teapot teiera **f**
tear (n) rottura **f**
tear (vb) rompere
teaspoon cucchiaino (da tè)
teat tettarella **f**
teeth denti **mpl**
telephone telefono **m**
telephone call chiamata
television televisione **f**
tell dire
temperature temperatura **f**
temple (anat) tempia **f**
temple (rel) tempio **m**
temporary temporaneo/a
tendon tendine **m**
tennis tennis **m**
tennis court campo da tennis
tennis racket racchetta da tennis
tent tenda **f**
tent peg piolo da tenda
terminal terminale
thank ringraziare
that quello, quel
the il, la , lo, i, gli, le

ENGLISH → ITALIAN

theatre teatro **m**
theft furto **m**
there là
thermometer termometro **m**
they loro
thick spesso/a
thief ladro/a **m/f**
thigh coscia **f**
thin sottile
thing cosa **f**
think pensare
third-party insurance assicurazione per terzi
thirsty assetato/a
this questo
this morning stamattina
this way da questa parte
this week questa settimana
thorn spina **f**
those quelli, quei, quegli
thousand mille **m**
thread filo **m**
throat gola **f**
throat lozenges pastiglie per la gola
through attraverso
throw gettare
thumb pollice **m**
thunder tuono **m**
thunderstorm temporale **m**
Thursday giovedì **m**
ticket biglietto **m**
ticket collector controllore **m**
ticket office biglietteria **f**
tide marea
tie cravatta **f**
tight stretto/a
tights collant **m**
till (cash register) cassa **f**
till (until) fino a
time ora
timetable orario **m**
tin barattolo **m**
tin opener apriscatole
tinfoil stagnola **f**
tiny minuscolo/a
tip mancia **f**
tired stanco/a
tissue fazzolettino di carta
to a
today oggi **m**
toe dito del piede **m**
together insieme
toilet toilette, gabinetto **m**
toll pedaggio
toll road strada a pedaggio
tomato pomodoro **m**
tomato juice succo di pomodoro
tomorrow domani
tomorrow afternoon domani pomeriggio
tomorrow evening domani sera

tomorrow morning domani mattina
tongue lingua **f**
tonight stasera, questa sera **f**
tonsillitis tonsillite **f**
too anche
tool attrezzo **m**
toolkit borsa arnesi
tooth dente **m**
toothache mal di denti
toothbrush spazzolino da denti
toothpick stuzzicadente
top tappo **m**
top floor ultimo piano
topless senza reggiseno
torch torcia **f**
torn bucato/a
total totale **m**
tough duro/a
tour giro **m**
tour guide guida **f**
tour operator operatore turistico **m**
tow rimorchiare
towel asciugamano **m**
tower torre **f**
town città **f**
town hall municipio **m**
toy giocattolo **m**
tracksuit tuta da ginnastica **f**
traffic traffico **m**
traffic jam ingorgo **m**
traffic light semaforo **m**
trailer rimorchio **m**
train treno **m**
tram tram **m**
tranquillizer tranquillante **m**
translate tradurre
translation traduzione **f**
translator traduttore **m**
trash spazzatura **f**
travel viaggiare
travel agent agente di viaggio
travel documents documenti di viaggio
travel sickness mal d'auto, d'aereo, di nave
traveller's cheque assegni per viaggiatori
tray vassoio **m**
tree albero **m**
trolley carrello **m**
trouble guaio **m**
trousers pantaloni **m**
trout trota **f**
truck camion **m**
true vero/a
trunk baule **m**
try provare
try on provarsi
tuna tonno **m**
tunnel galleria **f**
Turk, Turkish (n, adj) turco/a **m/f**
Turkey Turchia **f**
turkey tacchino **m**

turn girare
turn around girarsi
turn off spegnere
turquoise turchese
tweezers pinzette **f**
twice due volte
twin beds letti gemelli **m**
twins gemelli
type tipo **m**
typical tipico/a
tyre gomma **f**
tyre pressure pressione delle gomme

U

ugly brutto/a
U.K. Regno Unito **m**
ulcer ulcera f
umbrella ombrello **m**
uncle zio **m**
uncomfortable scomodo/a
unconscious privo di sensi
under sotto
underdone al sangue
underground sottoterra
underpants mutande **f**
understand capire
underwear biancheria intima **f**
unemployed disoccupato
United States Stati Uniti (d'America)
university università **f**
unleaded petrol benzina senza piombo
unlimited illimitato/a
unlock aprire con la chiave
unpack disfare le valigie
unscrew svitare
until fino a
unusual insolito/a
up su
upmarket di qualità
upside down sottosopra
upstairs al piano di sopra
urgent urgente
us noi
use usare
useful utile
usual usuale
usually di solito

V

vacancy posto vacante
vacation vacanza **f**
vaccination vaccinazione **f**
vacuum cleaner aspirapolvere **m**
valid valido/a
valley valle **f**
valuable di valore
value (n) valore **m**
value (vb) valutare
valve valvola **f**
van furgone **m**

ENGLISH → ITALIAN

vanilla vaniglia **f**
VAT imposta sul valore aggiunto
veal vitello **m**
vegetables verdure **f**
vegetarian vegetariano **m**
vehicle veicolo **m**
vein vena **f**
vending machine distributore automatico
venereal disease malattia venerea **f**
very molto/a
vest maglia (della pelle)
vet (veterinarian) veterinario **m**
via via
Vienna Vienna **f**
view vista **f**
village villaggio **m**
vinegar aceto **m**
vineyard vigneto **m**
violet violetto **f**
virus virus **m**
visa visto **m**
visit (n) visita **f**
visit (vb) visitare
visiting hours orario delle visite
visitor ospite **m/f**
voice voce **f**
volcano vulcano **m**
voltage voltaggio **m**
vomit vomitare
voucher buono **m**

W
wage salario **m**
waist vita **f**
waistcoat panciotto **m**
wait aspettare
waiter/waitress cameriere/a **m/f**
waiting room sala d'aspetto
wake up svegliarsi
wake-up call chiamata di sveglia
Wales Galles **m**
walk (n) camminata **f,** passeggiata **f**
walk (vb) camminare
wall muro **m**
wallet portafoglio **m**
walnut noce **f**
want volere
war guerra **f**
ward (hospital) padiglione **m,** corsia **f**
wardrobe guardaroba **f**
warehouse magazzino **m**
warm caldo/a
wash lavare
washbasin lavandino **m**
washing powder detersivo **m**
washing-up liquid detersivo per i piatti
wasp vespa **f**
waste (n) scarto **m**
waste (vb) sprecare
waste bin pattumiera **f**
watch (n) orologio **m**

ENGLISH → ITALIAN

watch (vb) guardare
watch strap cinturino dell'orologio
water acqua **f**
watermelon anguria **f**
waterproof impermeabile
waterskiing sci acquatico
wave onda **f**
way percorso **m**
we noi
weak debole
wear portare
weather tempo **m**
weather forecast previsioni del tempo
web ragnatela **f**
wedding matrimonio **m**
wedding present regalo di nozze
wedding ring fede **f**
Wednesday mercoledì **m**
week settimana
weekday giorno feriale
weekend fine settimana
weekly settimanale
weigh pesare
weight peso **m**
weird misterioso/a
welcome benvenuto
well bene
Welsh gallese
were erano
west ovest **m**
wet bagnato/a
whale balena **f**
What? Cosa?
What is wrong? Che cosa non va?
What's the time? Che ora è?
wheel ruota **f**
wheel clamp ceppo bloccaruote
wheelchair sedia a rotelle
When? Quando?
Where? Dove?
Which? Quale?
while mentre
whipped cream panna montata **f**
white bianco/a
Who? Chi?
whole tutto/a, intero/a
wholemeal bread pane integrale
Whose? Di chi?
Why? Perchè
wide largo/a
widow vedova **f**
widower vedovo **m**
wife moglie **f**
wig parrucca **f**
win vincere
wind vento **m**
window finestra **f**
window seat posto al finestrino
windscreen parabrezza
windscreen wiper tergicristallo **m**
windy ventoso/a
wine vino **m**

wine list lista dei vini
winter inverno **m**
wire filo metallico **m**
wish (n) desiderio **m**
wish (vb) desiderare
with con
without senza
witness testimone **m/f**
wolf lupo **m**
woman donna **f**
wood legno **m,** bosco **m**
wool lana **f**
word parola **f**
work (n) lavoro **m**
work (vb) lavorare
world mondo **m**
worried preoccupato/a
worse peggio/a
worth valore **m**
wrap up avvolgere
wrapping paper carta da imballaggio
wrinkles rughe **f**
wrist polso **m**
write scrivere
writing paper carta da lettere **f**
wrong sbagliato/a

X

X-ray raggi-X **m**

Y

yacht panfilo **m**
year anno **m**
yellow giallo **m**
yellow pages pagine gialle
yes si
yesterday ieri
yolk tuorlo **m**
you tu, voi
young giovane
your il tuo, il vostro
youth hostel ostello della gioventù

Z

zero zero **m**
zipper, zip fastener cerniera **f**
zone zona **f**
zoo zoo **m**, giardino zoologico

A
a at, to
a buon mercato cheap
a più buon mercato cheaper
a strisce striped
abbaiare bark (vb, dog)
abbastanza f enough
abbazia f abbey
abbonamento m season ticket
abbondanza f plenty
abbronzato/a suntanned
abbronzatura f tan
aborto m abortion
accanto beside
acceleratore m accelerator
accendere switch on
accendino m cigarettelighter
accensione f ignition
accento m accent
accettare accept
accettazione bagagli check in
acchiappare catch
acclamazione f cheering
accordarsi agree
accordo m agreement
aceto m vinegar
acetone nail polish remover
acqua f water
acqua dentifricia f mouthwash
acqua di colonia f cologne
acqua minerale mineral water
acqua potabile drinking water
adattatore m adapter
aderire stick (vb)
adesso now
adulto m, adulta f adult
aeroplano m plane, aeroplane
aeroporto m airport
affare m business
affettare slice (vb)
affittare hire, lease, rent (vb)
affittare una macchina car hire
affitto m rent (n)
affollato/a crowded
affrancatura f postage
affrettare hurry, rush (vb)
agenda f diary
agente di viaggio travel agent
agente immobiliare estate agent
aggiustare fix

aggredito/a e derubato/a mugged
aglio m garlic
agnello m lamb
ago m needle
ago ipodermico hypodermic needle
agricoltore m farmer
agro/a sour
aiutare help (vb)
Aiuto! Help!
al piano di sopra upstairs
al piano di sotto downstairs
al sangue underdone
alba f dawn, sunrise
albero m mast, tree
alcuni a few, some
alga marina f seaweed
alimenti per l'infanzia baby food
aliscafo m hydrofoil
all'aperto outdoors
all'estero abroad
all'inizio at first
alla griglia grilled
allacciare fasten
allacciare la cintura di sicurezza fasten seatbelt
alloggio m accommodation
alloggio prima colazione bed & breakfast
alluvione f flood
alpinismo m mountaineering
alta marea high tide
altalena f swing
altezza f height
alto/a high, tall
altrimenti otherwise
altro/a other
alzarsi get up
amare love (vb)
ambasciata f embassy
ambra f amber
ambulanza f ambulance
amica f friend, girlfriend
amichevole friendly
amico m friend, boyfriend
amico di penna penfriend
ammalato/a sick
ammortizzatore m shock absorber
amore m love (n)
analcolico m non-alcoholic
analgesico m painkiller
ananas m pineapple
anatra f duck
anche also, too
ancora still
andare go
andare a prendere fetch

andare a visitare posti sightseeing
andare in pensione retired
andarsene go away
anello m ring (n)
anestesia f anaesthetic
angolo m corner
anguilla f eel
anguria f watermelon
animale m animal
animale domestico m pet
anniversario m anniversary
anno m year
Anno Nuovo New Year
annuale annual
anteriore front
antiacido antacid
anticipatamente in advance
anticipo m advance
antico/a ancient
anticoncezionale contraceptive
antimeridiane a.m. (before noon)
antipasto m starter (meal)
antiquato/a old-fashioned
anziano m senior citizen
ape f bee
aperto/a open
apparecchio acustico hearing aid
appartamento m flat (n), apartment
appartato/a secluded
appena hardly, just
appendicite f appendicitis
appuntamento m appointment, date
apribottiglie m bottle opener
aprire con la chiave unlock
apriscatole f can opener, tin opener
aquila f eagle
arachide m peanut
aragosta f lobster
arancia f orange
area f area
argento m silver
aria f air
aria condizionata air conditioning
armadietto m locker
armadio m cupboard
arrabbiato/a angry, cross
arrampicarsi climb
arrestare arrest (vb)
arresto m arrest (n)
arrivederci goodbye
arrivo m arrival
arrugginito/a rusty
arte f art, craft
artista f artist

ascensore m lift (n), elevator)
ascesso m abscess
asciugacapelli hairdryer
asciugamano m towel
asciugare con l'asciugacapelli blow-dry
asciugatore dryer
asciutto/a dry
ascoltare listen
asilo m crèche
aspettare wait, expect
aspettarsi expect
aspirapolvere m vacuum cleaner
assaggiare taste (vb)
assalire attack (vb)
asse da stiro ironing board
assegni per viaggiatori traveller's cheque
assegno m cheque
assetato/a thirsty
assicurazione f insurance
assicurazione per la macchina car insurance
assicurazione per terzi third-party insurance
assicurazione sanitaria medical insurance
assicurazione sulla vita life insurance
assolato/a sunny
assolutamente absolutely
assonnato/a sleepy
assorbenti igienici m sanitary pads
atrio m lobby
attaccapanni m hanger, coat hanger
attaccare attack (vb)
attacco m attack (n)
attraverso through
attrezzatura f equipment
attrezzo m tool
autista f driver
autobus m bus
autolavaggio car wash
autostrada f freeway, motorway
autunno m autumn
avena f oats
avere have
avviatore m starter (car)
avvisare advise
avvitare screw (vb)
avvocato m lawyer
avvolgere wrap up

B

baciare kiss (vb)
bacio m kiss (n)
badare look after, take care, mind (vb)
baffi m moustache

ITALIAN → ENGLISH

ITALIAN → ENGLISH

bagaglio m baggage, luggage
bagaglio a mano hand luggage
bagaglio in eccedenza excess luggage
bagnato/a wet
bagnino m life guard
bagno m bath
baia f bay
balcone m balcony
balena f whale
ballare dance (vb)
bambinaia f nanny
bambino m child
bambola f doll
bancarelle f stalls
banchina f quay
banco m counter, desk
bandiera f flag
bar omosessuale gay bar
barattolo m jar, tin
barba f beard
barbiere m barber
barile m barrel
bassa marea low tide
basso/a low
bastone m stick (n)
batteria scarica flat battery
baule m trunk
Baviera Bavaria
Belgio m Belgium
bello/a beautiful, nice, handsome, lovely
benchè although
benda f bandage
bene well
benvenuto welcome
benzina f petrol, gas
benzina senza piombo lead-free/ unleaded petrol
bere drink (vb)
bernoccolo m lump
berretto m cap
bestemmia f swear word
bestemmiare swear (curse)
bevanda f drink (n)
biancheria f lingerie
biancheria intima f underwear
bianco/a white
bibita analcolica f soft drink
biblioteca f library
bicchiere m glass
bicicletta f bicycle
bidone m bin
biglietteria f ticket office
biglietto m ticket
biglietto aereo m air ticket
biglietto aperto m open ticket
biglietto di andata single ticket

biglietto di andata e ritorno return ticket
biglietto di auguri (di compleanno) (birthday) card
bilancia f scale
binario m platform
binocoli binoculars
biondo/a fair (hair colour)
birra f lager
birra alla spina draught beer
birreria brewery **f**
biscotto m biscuit, cookie
bisognare need (vb)
bisogno m need (n)
bloccato blocked
blocco di appartamenti m block of flats
blu blue
blu marino m navy blue
bocca f mouth
boccale m mug
bollire boil (vb)
bollitore (per l'acqua) kettle
bombolone doughnut
bordo m edge
borsa f bag, handbag
borsa arnesi toolkit
borsa per acqua calda hot-water bottle
borsa per la spesa carrier bag
borsa termica f cool bag/box
borsaiolo m pickpocket
borsellino m purse
bosco m wood
bottiglia f bottle
bottone m button
braccialetto m bracelet
brezza f breeze
brillante bright
brocca f jug
bronchite f bronchitis
bruciare burn (vb)
bruciatura f burn (n)
brutto/a awful, ugly
Bruxelles Brussels
buca f pothole
buca per le lettere letterbox
bucato/a torn
bucato m laundry
buccia f peel (n)
buco m hole
bugia f lie (n, untruth)
bulbo m bulb (plant)
Buon Anno Nuovo! Happy New Year!
buon giorno good afternoon, good day, good morning
Buona fortuna! Good luck!

ITALIAN → ENGLISH

Buona Pasqua! Happy Easter!
buona sera good evening
buonanotte good night
buono m voucher
buono/a good
burro m butter
bussare knock
bussola f compass
busta f envelope
busta di carta carrier bag
bustina di tè teabag

C
cabina f cabin
cabina telefonica f phone booth
cacao m cocoa
caccia f hunt (n)
cacciare hunt (vb)
cacciavite m screwdriver
cadere fall
caffè m coffee
caffè ghiacciato iced coffee
caffè solubile instant coffee
calce f lime
calcio m kick (n), football
calcolatrice f calculator
caldo/a hot, warm
calmo/a calm
calore m heat
calza f stocking
calzini m socks
calzoncini corti shorts
cambiare change (vb)
cambiavalute bureau de change
cambio di velocità gearbox
camera f room
camera con colazione bed & breakfast
camera d'aria f inner tube
camera da bagno bathroom
camera doppia double room
camera singola single room
cameriera f maid, chambermaid
cameriere/a m/f waiter/waitress
camerino m dressing room, changing room
camicetta f blouse
camicia f shirt
camicia da notte nightdress
camino m chimney
camion m truck, lorry
camminare walk (vb)
camminata f walk (n)
camoscio m suede

campagna f countryside
campanello m bell
campanello della porta doorbell
campeggiare camp (vb)
campeggio m campsite
campeggio per carovane caravan site
campo m field
campo da tennis tennis court
campo di golf golf course
Canada Canada
canale m canal, channel
cancellare cancel
cancellazione cancellation
cancello m gate
cancro m cancer
candela f candle, spark plug
cane m dog
canna da pesca fishing rod
canoa f canoe
canotto pneumatico dinghy
cantante m/f singer
cantare sing
cantina f cellar
canzone f song
capelli m hair
capire understand
capitale f capital (city)
capitale m capital (money)
capo m head
cappella f chapel
cappello m hat
cappotto m coat, overcoat
cappuccio m hood (of garment)
capra f goat
caramella f candy
carbone m coal
carbone di legna m charcoal
carburante fuel
carburatore m carburettor
cardigan m cardigan
carello portabagagli luggage trolley
caricare charge
carino/a pretty
carne f meat
carne di maiale pork
carne di montone mutton
caro/a dear, expensive
carota f carrot
carovana f caravan
carrello m trolley
carro attrezzi/ soccorso breakdown van
carrozza f carriage

carrozzella f pram
carta f paper
carta assegni cheque card
carta avvolgente adesiva f cling film
carta d'identità identity card
carta d'imbarco boarding card
carta da imballaggio wrapping paper
carta da lettere f writing paper, notepaper
carta di credito charge card, credit card
carta geografica f map
carta stradale f road map
cartella f briefcase
cartello stradale m road sign
cartoleria f stationer's
cartolina f postcard
cartone m cardboard
casa f house, home
casa colonica farmhouse
casco m helmet, crash helmet
cassa f till, cash register, cash desk
cassetta f cassette
cassetta delle lettere post box
cassetta di pronto soccorso first-aid kit
cassetto m drawer
cassettone m chest of drawers
cassiere/a m/f cashier
castagna f **chestnut**
castello m castle
cattedrale f cathedral
cattivo/a bad, nasty
cattolico/a m/f Catholic
cauto/a careful
cavalcare ride (vb)
cavalcata f ride (n)
cavallo m horse
cavatappi m corkscrew
cavi con morsetti jump leads
caviglia f ankle
cavolfiore m cauliflower
cavolo m cabbage
CE f EC
cena f dinner, supper
centigrado m Centigrade
centimetro m centimetre
centralinista m/f operator (phone)
centrifuga f spin-dryer
centro m centre
centro commerciale m shopping centre
centro della città city centre

ceppo bloccaruote wheel clamp
ceramica f pottery
cercare look for
cerchio m circle
cerniera f zipper, zip fastener
cerotto m sticking plaster
certamente certainly
certificato m certificate
certificato di nascita birth certificate
certo/a certain, sure
cespuglio m bush
cestino m basket
cetriolo m cucumber
champagne m champagne
Che cosa c'è? What's the matter
Che cosa non va? What is wrong?
che lavora in proprio self-employed
Che ora è? What's the time?
Chi? Who?
chiamare call (vb)
chiamata f call (n), telephone call
chiamata a carico del destinatario reverse-charge call
chiamata di sveglia wake-up call
chiamata interurbana long-distance call
chiaro/a clear, light (adj, not dark)
chiave f key
chiave dell' accensione ignition key
chiave inglese spanner
chiavi per la macchina car keys
chiesa f church
chilo m kilo
chilogrammo m kilogram
chilometro m kilometre
chiosco m kiosk
chirurgia f surgery (procedure)
chitarra f guitar
chiudere close, shut, lock (vb)
chiudere dentro lock in
chiudere fuori lock out
chiunque anybody
cibo m food
cibo per bambini baby food
ciclo m cycle
cieco/a blind (adj)
cielo m sky
ciliegia f cherry
cilindro a gas gas cylinder

ITALIAN → ENGLISH

cima f summit
cimitero m cemetery
Cina f China
cinema m cinema
cinghia f strap
cinghia del ventilatore fan belt
cinghiale m boar
cintura f belt
cintura di sicurezza f seat belt, safety belt
cintura portasoldi money belt
cinturino dell'orologio watch strap
cioccolato m chocolate
cipolla f onion
circa about (approximately)
circolo m del golf golf club (place)
circondato surrounded
circonvallazione f ring road, bypass
ciste f cyst
cisterna f cistern
cistite f cystitis
città f city, town
cittadino/a m/f citizen
clacson m horn (car)
classe f class
classe economia economy class
classificare sort (vb)
clavicola f collar bone
cliente m client, customer
clinica f clinic
Coca-cola f Coke
codice m code
codice postale postal code
cofano m hood, bonnet (of car)
cognac m brandy
cognata f sister-in-law
cognato m brother-in-law
cognome m surname
cognome da nubile maiden name
coincidenza f connection
coito m sex (intercourse)
colatoio m colander
colla f glue
collana f necklace
collant m pantyhose, tights
collega colleague
colletto m collar
collezionare collect
collo m neck
colluttorio m mouthwash
colore m colour
colpo m hit, stroke (n)
coltello m knife
come like (prep)
Come? How?

Come stai? How are you?
cominciare start
commedia f comedy
commesso m shop assistant
commissariato m police station
commozione cerebrale concussion
comodo/a comfortable, convenient
compagnia f company
compagno/a m/f partner (companion)
comperare buy
compilare fill in
compitare spell (vb, grammar)
compleanno m birthday
completamente completely, quite
compositore m composer
comprare buy
computer m computer
con with
con giustizia fairly
con speranza hopefully
concerto m concert
concessione f concession
condimento m dressing, seasoning
condimento per insalata salad dressing
condizione f condition
condurre lead (vb)
conferenza f conference
conferma f confirmation
confermare confirm
confondere confuse, mix up
congelato frozen
congelatore m freezer
congestionato jammed
congiungimento m junction
congratulazioni congratulations
coniglio m rabbit
conscio/a conscious
consegna f delivery
consegnare deliver
consolato m consulate
contatore m meter
contatto m contact (n)
contento/a glad
continuare continue
conto m account, bill
contorno m side dish

ITALIAN → ENGLISH

contraccettivo contraceptive
contratto m contract
contratto d'affitto m lease (n)
contro against
controllo m pass control
controllore m ticket collector
coperchio m lid
coperta f blanket
coperto m cover charge
copiare copy
coppia f couple
corda f rope, string
corda del bucato clothes line
cornice f frame, picture frame
corno m horn (car)
coro m choir
corona f crown
corpo m body
corrente current (adj)
corrente f current (n)
corrente d'aria draught
correre run
correttamente properly
corretto/a correct, right
corridoio m aisle, corridor
corriere courier service
corsa f race (sport)
corse di cavalli horse racing
corsia f ward (hospital)
corso m course
corso di lingua language course
corteccia m bark (n, of tree)
cortese polite
cortile m playground
corto/a short
cosa f thing
Cosa? What?
coscia f thigh
costa f coast
costo m cost
costola f rib
costoletta f chop (n)
costruire build
costume da bagno m swimming costume
cotone m cotton
cotone idrofilo cotton wool
cozze fpl mussels
crampo m cramp
cravatta f tie
cravatta a farfalla bow tie
credere believe
crema idratante moisturizer
crema pasticciera custard

crema solare sun block
cricco m jack
crimine m crime
cristallo m crystal
crociera f cruise
crollare collapse
crudo/a raw
cuccetta f couchette
cucchiaino (da tè) teaspoon
cucchiaio m spoon
cucchiaio (da tavola) tablespoon
cucina f kitchen
cucina a gas gas cooker
cucinare cook (vb)
cucinino m kitchenette
cucire sew
cuffia fpl earphones
cuffie headphones
cugino m cousin
cuoco m chef, cook (n)
cuore m heart
cupo/a dull
curva f bend
cuscino m cushion
custode m/f caretaker

D

da by (e.g. author), from, like (prep)
da qualche parte somewhere
da questa parte this way
da solo by myself (alone)
dado m dice, nut (for bolt)
daltonico colour blind
danaroso/a posh
Danimarca f Denmark
danno m damage (n)
dappertutto everywhere
dare give
dare fastidio annoy
data di nascita date of birth
data di scadenza f sell-by date
datteri m dates
davvero really
debiti m debts
debole weak
decaffeinato decaffeinated
decidere decide
decisione f decision
decolorante m bleach
dedurre deduct
del mattino a.m. (before noon)
del pomeriggio p.m. (after noon)
deliberatamente deliberately
delizioso/a delicious
deluso/a disappointed
denaro contante cash

dente m tooth
denti mpl teeth
dentiera dentures
dentista m/f dentist
dentro indoors
dentro a into
depositare deposit (vb)
deposito m deposit (n)
descrivere describe
descrizione description **f**
desiderare wish (vb)
desiderio m wish (n)
destro/a right (direction)
destinazione f destination
detergente cleaning solution
detergente per trucco eye make-up remover
detersivo m washing powder, detergent
detersivo in polvere soap powder
detersivo per i piatti washing-up liquid
deviazione f detour
di of
Di chi? Whose?
di mezzo m middle
di moda fashionable
di nuovo again
di prim'ordine first class
di qualità upmarket
di seconda second-hand (used)
di taglia media medium sized
di valore valuable
diabetico/a m/f diabetic (adj, n)
diamante m diamond
diarrea f diarrhoea
dicembre m December
dieta f diet
dietro behind
difetto m fault, flaw
difettoso/a faulty
differenza f difference
difficile difficult
dimenticare forget
dinamo f dynamo
Dio m God
dire say, tell
diretto/a direct
direttore m manager
direzione f direction
diritto/a straight
disastro m disaster
disco m disk
disco parcheggio m parking disc
disco rigido hard disk
disegno m drawing, pattern, picture
disfare le valigie unpack
disinfettante m disinfectant

disoccupato unemployed
dispari odd (of numbers)
disponibile available
disseminare litter (vb)
distanza f distance
distributore automatico vending machine
disturbare disturb
dito m finger
dito del piede m toe
divano m couch
diverso/a different
divertente funny
divertimento m fun
divertirsi enjoy
dividere share (vb)
divo/a m/f star (film)
divorziato/a divorced
dizionario m dictionary
doccia f shower
documenti di viaggio travel documents
documento m document, record (n)
dogana f customs
dolce sweet (adj)
dolce m dessert, pudding
dolorante sore
dolore m ache, pain
doloroso/a painful
domanda f enquiry, question (n)
domandare ask, question (vb)
domani tomorrow
domani mattina tomorrow morning
domani pomeriggio tomorrow afternoon
domani sera tomorrow evening
domenica f Sunday
domestico/a domestic
donna f woman
donna poliziotta policewoman
dopo after
doppio/a double
dormire sleep
dottore m doctor
Dove? Where?
dovere should, must, owe
dovuto due
dozzina f dozen
dramma m play (n, theatre)
droga f drug (med)
drogheria f food shop
due volte twice
durante during
duro/a hard, tough

E

e and
è is

ITALIAN → ENGLISH

ITALIAN → ENGLISH

È un peccato It's a pity
ebraico/a Jewish
ebreo m Jew
eccellente excellent
eccetto except
eccitante exciting
economia f economy
edicola f news stand
edificio m building
elastico/a elastic
elenco telefonico m phonebook
elettricista electrician
elettricità f electricity
elettrico/a electric
elicottero m helicopter
emergenza f emergency
emicrania f migraine
entrare come in, enter
entrata f entrance
entrata forzata break in
entro le by (time)
epilettico/a m/s epileptic (adj, n)
equitazione (del cavallo) horse riding
erano were
erba cipollina chives
erba f grass, herbs
ernia f hernia
errore m error
eruzione f rash
esame m examination
esattamente exactly
esausto/a exhausted
esca f bait
escludere exclude
escursione f excursion
escursione con guida guided tour
esecuzione f performance
esempio m example
esente da dogana duty-free
esperto/a experienced
esplosione f explosion
esportare export
esposizione f exposure
espresso/a express
essenziale essential
essere be
essere impaziente di look forward to
est east
estate f summer
esterno m outside
estintore m fire extinguisher
Estonia Estonia
estraneo m stranger
età f age
etichetta f label

etichetta per bagagli luggage tag
Europa f Europe
europeo/a m/f European (adj, n)
evitare avoid

F

fa ago
fa male it's sore
fabbrica f factory
faccenda f matter
faccia f face
facile easy
fagiolo m bean
falegname m carpenter
falena f moth
falso/a false, fake
famiglia f family
famoso/a famous
fango m mud
far male hurt
far pagare più del dovuto overcharged
fare do, make
fare deltaplano m hang-gliding
fare il check-in check in
fare jogging jog
fare l'autostop hitchhike
fare una foto to take a photo
farfalla f butterfly
fari mpl headlights
farina f flour
farmacia f pharmacy
farmacista f chemist
fasciatura f dressing (bandage)
fatto/a made
fatto a mano handmade
fattoria f farm
fattura f invoice
fax fax
fazzolettino di carta tissue
fazzoletto m handkerchief
febbraio m February
febbre f fever
fede f wedding ring
federa f pillowcase
fegato m liver
felice happy
femmina f female
ferita f injury
ferito/a injured
fermare stop (vb)
fermare con una graffa staple
fermata f stop (n)
fermata d'autobus bus stop
ferro da calza knitting needle
ferro da stiro iron
ferrovia f railway
festa f festival, party (celebration)

festa nazionale public holiday
festival m festival
fetta f slice (n)
fiammiferi mpl matches (for lighting)
fianco m hip
fiasco m flask
fidanzato/a m/f fiancé, fiancée
fidanzato/a engaged (to be married)
fiera f fair (fête)
figlia f daughter
figlio m son
fila f queue, row (n)
filetto m fillet
film m film
filo m thread
filo metallico m wire
filtro m filter
filza f file (folder)
finalmente eventually
fine f end (n)
fine settimana weekend
finestra f window
finire finish, end (vb)
fino a until, till
fioraio m florist
fiore m flower
firma f signature
firmare sign (vb)
fiume m river
flanella f flannel
fluente fluent
fluido fluent
fodera duvet cover
foglia f leaf
foglia d'alloro bay leaf
folla f crowd
fontana f fountain
foratura f puncture
forbici f scissors
forbicine da unghie nail scissors
forchetta f fork
foresta f forest
Foresta Nera Black Forest
forestiero m foreigner
formaggio m cheese
formale formal
formica f ant
fornello m cooker
forno m oven
forno a microonde microwave
forse maybe, perhaps
forte loud, strong
fortezza f fortress
fortuna f luck
fortunatamente fortunately
fortunato/a lucky
foruncolo m boil (n, med)
foschia f mist
fossa biologica/settica f septic tank
foto f photo

fotocopia f photocopy
fragile breakable
fragola f strawberry
frana f landslide
francese French
francese m/f Frenchman/woman
Francia f France
francobollo m stamp, postage stamp
frase f sentence (grammar)
fratello m brother
frattura f fracture
freccia f indicator
freddo/a cold
freno m brake
freno a mano handbrake
frequente frequent
fresco/a cool, fresh
fretta quickly
fretta f hurry, rush (n)
friggere fry
frigo m fridge
frittata f omelette
frittella f pancake
fritto fried
frizione f clutch
frizzante fizzy, sparkling
frode f rip-off
fronte f forehead
frontiera f border
frutta f fruit
frutti di mare shellfish
fruttivendolo m greengrocer
fuga f escape (n)
fumare smoke (vb)
fumo m smoke (n)
funerale m funeral
fungo m mushroom
funicolare f funicular
funivia f cable car
fuochi di Sant'Antonio shingles
fuoco m fire
fuori out
fuoristrada f four-wheel-drive vehicle
furgone m van
furto m burglary, theft
fusibile m fuse
futuro m future

G

gabbiano m seagull
gabinetto m lavatory, toilet
gabinetto medico f surgery, doctor's rooms
galleria f gallery, tunnel
Galles m Wales
gallese Welsh
gallone m gallon
gamba f leg
gamberetti mpl shrimps
gambero m prawn
garage m garage
garanzia f guarantee

ITALIAN → ENGLISH

gatto m cat
gelato m ice cream
gelo m frost
geloso/a jealous
gemelli twins
gemelli m cufflinks
generale general (adj)
genero m son-in-law
generoso/a generous
genitori m parents
gennaio m January
gente f folk
gentile kind (adj)
genuino/a genuine
gesso m plaster
gettare throw
ghiacciaio m glacier
ghiaccio m ice
ghiaia f shingle
già already
giacca f jacket
giacere lie (vb, recline)
giallo m yellow
giardino m garden
giardino zoologico zoo
Ginevra f Geneva
ginocchio m knee
giocare play (vb)
giocattolo m toy
gioco m play (n), game
gioia f joy
gioielleria f jeweller's
gioielli m jewellery
giornale m newspaper
giornaliero/a daily
giorno m day
giorno feriale weekday
giostra f roundabout
giovane young
giovedì m Thursday
girare turn
girarsi turn around
giro m tour
giubbotto di salvataggio life jacket
giudicare judge (vb)
giudice judge (n)
giugno m June
giuntura f joint
giunzione f junction
giurare swear (an oath)
giusto/a fair, just, right
gli the
goccia f drop (n)
goccie per gli occhi eye drops
gola f throat
golf m jumper
gomito m elbow
gomma f rubber, tyre
gomma a terra flat tyre
gomma da masticare chewing gum
gonfiare swell
gonfio/a swollen
gonfiore m swelling
gonna skirt
gotico/a Gothic
governo government

gradino step
grado m degree (measurement)
gradualment gradually
graffiare scratch (vb)
graffio m scratch (n)
grammatica grammar
grammo gram
Gran Bretagna Great Britain
granaio barn
granchio m crab
grande big, great, large
grande magazzino m department store
grandine f hail
grandioso/a grand
grappolo m bunch (grapes)
grasso/a fat, fatty, greasy
grassoccio/a fatty
grato/a grateful
grattugiare grate
Grecia f Greece
greco m Greek (adj, n)
grembiule m apron
gridare shout (vb)
grido m shout (n)
grigio/a grey
grotta f cave
gruccia f coat hanger
gruppo m group
guaio m trouble
guancia f cheek
guanciale m pillow
guanti m gloves
guardare look at, watch (vb)
guardaroba f cloakroom, wardrobe
guardia f guard
guardia costiera coastguard
guardia di sicurezza security guard
guardiano m caretaker
guasto out of order
guasto m breakdown (car)
guerra f war
gufo m owl
guida f guide (n), tour guide
guida a destra right-hand drive
guida telefonica directory (phone)
guida turistica guide book
guidare drive
gusto m taste (n)

H

hamburger hamburger
handicappato/a handicapped
ho fame I am hungry
Ho voglia di vomitare! I'm going to be sick!
hovercraft m hovercraft

I

i the
idea f idea
idraulico m plumber
ieri yesterday
ieri notte last night
ieri sera last night
il the
il mio m my
il suo his
il tuo your
il vostro your
illimitato/a unlimited
imitazione f fake (n)
immediatamente immediately
immersioni subacquee scuba diving
immondizia f rubbish, refuse (n)
imparare learn
impermeabile waterproof (adj)
impermeabile m raincoat
impiegato ricezione receptionist
importante important
impossibile impossible
imposta sul valore aggiunto VAT
impostare mail, post (vb)
improvvisamente suddenly
in in
in buona salute fit, healthy
in discesa downhill
in fondo alla at the bottom
in modo imparziale fairly
in seguito afterwards
in tutto altogether
in un appartamento attrezzato di cucina self-catering
incantesimo m spell (n, magic)
inceppato stuck
inchiostro m ink
incidente m accident, road accident
incinta pregnant
incluso included
incontrare meet
incontro m match (n, game), meeting
incredibile incredible, amazing
incrocio m crossroads
indiano/a m/f Indian (adj, n)
indicare point (vb)
indicatore della benzina fuel gauge
indigestione f indigestion
indipendente freelance
infarto heart attack

infenzione f infection
infermiera, infermiere nurse, male nurse
infettivo/a infectious
infiammazione f inflammation
influenza f flu
informale informal
informazione f information
infradito flip flops
ingegnere m engineer
Inghilterra England
inghiottire swallow
inglese English
inglese m/f Englishman/woman
ingorgo m traffic jam
ingrandimento m enlargement
ingredienti mpl ingredients
iniezione f injection
inquinato polluted
insalata f salad
insegnante m/f teacher
insegnare teach
insettifugo m insect repellent
insetto m insect
insieme together
insistere insist
insolazione f sunstroke
insolito/a unusual
insonnia f insomnia
insulina f insulin
intelligente intelligent, clever
intelligenza f mind (n)
intendere mean (vb, intend)
interdentale dental floss
interessante interesting
internazionale international
interno inside
intero/a whole
interprete m/f interpreter
interruttore m switch
interruttore principale mains switch
interruzione di corrente power cut
intersezione f intersection
intervallo m interval
intossicazione alimentare food poisoning
invalido/a disabled
invece instead
inverno m winter
invertire reverse
investire knock down
invitare invite
invito m invitation
io I
io sono I am
io stesso myself

ITALIAN → ENGLISH

ippodromo m race course
Irlanda f Ireland
Irlanda del Nord f Northern Ireland
irlandese Irish
irlandese m/f Irishman/woman
isola f island
istituto di bellezza beauty salon
Italia f Italy
italiano/a m/f Italian (adj, n)
itterizia f jaundice

L
la the
la f it
là there, over there
l'abbigliamento da donna ladies wear
l'abbigliamento da uomo menswear
l'ufficio postale principale main post office
l'uno o l'altro either of them
la mia f my
laccio m, laccio da scarpa shoe lace
ladro/a m/f burglar, thief
lago m lake
Lago di Garda Lake Garda
Lago Maggiore Lake Maggiore
lamentarsi complain
lamentela f complaint
lamette da barba razor blades
lampada f lamp
lampadina f light bulb
lampo m flash, lightning
lampone m raspberry
lana f wool
lancetta dei secondi f second hand (of clock)
largo/a wide
lasciare leave
lasciarsi andare let off (oneself)
lassativo m laxative
lato m side
latta f can (n, tin)
latta per benzina f petrol can
latte m milk
latte in polvere powdered milk
lattina f can (n, tin)
lattuga f lettuce
laurea f degree (qualification)
lavanderia f launderette, laundromat
lavandino m sink, washbasin
lavare wash
lavastoviglie f dishwasher

lavorare work (vb)
lavorare a maglia knit
lavori stradali m roadworks
lavoro m job, work (n)
lavoro domestico housework
le the
lecca-lecca lollipop
legge f law
leggere read
leggero/a light (adj, not heavy)
legno m wood
lei her
lei f she
lentamente slowly
lente f lens
lente d'ingrandimento magnifying glass
lenti a contatto contact lens
lenticchie f lentils
lento/a slow
lenzuolo m sheet
leone m lion
lepre f hare
lesbica f lesbian
lettera f letter
letti gemelli m twin beds
lettino m cot
lettino portatile m carry-cot
letto m bed
letto matrimoniale double bed
letto singolo single bed
Lettonia f Latvia
lettore di compact CD player
leva f lever
leva del cambio gear lever
lezione f lesson
libbra f pound (weight)
libero/a free, loose
libreria f bookshop
libretto degli assegni cheque book
libro m book (n)
libro di fraseologia phrase book
licenza f licence
lieto/a pleased
lima f file (tool)
limetta da unghie f nail file
limite di velocità speed limit
limonata f lemonade
limone m lemon
lingua f language, tongue
lino m linen
liquido per freni brake fluid
liquore liqueur
lista f list
lista dei vini wine list
lite f quarrel (n)
litigare quarrel (vb)
litro m litre
Lituania f Lithuania

ITALIAN → ENGLISH

livido m bruise (n)
lo the
lo m it
locale local
locanda f inn
lontano/a far
loro they
lotta f fight (n)
lottare fight (vb)
lozione detergente cleansing lotion
lucchetto m padlock
luce f light (n)
luce del freno brake light
luce del sole sunshine
lucidare polish (vb)
lucido m polish (n)
luglio m July
lui he, him
luna f moon
luna di miele honeymoon
lunedì m Monday
lungamente long (adv)
lungo/a long (adj)
luogo di villeggiatura resort
lupo m wolf
Lussenburgo Luxembourg
lusso m luxury

M

ma but
macchia f stain
macchina f car, machine
macchina a noleggio hire car
macellaio m butcher
madre f mother
magazzino m store, warehouse
maggio m May
maggior parte di most
maglia f jersey
maglia (della pelle) vest
maglieria f knitwear
maglione m sweater, pullover
magnete m magnet
magro low fat
mai never
maiale m pig
maionese f mayonnaise
mal d'auto, d'aereo, di nave travel sickness
mal d'orecchi earache
mal di denti toothache
mal di gola sore throat
mal di mare seasickness
mal di schiena backache
mal di stomaco stomachache
mal di testa headache

malato/a ill
malattia f disease, illness
malattia venerea f venereal disease
malinteso m misunderstanding
mancante missing
mancare miss (vb)
mancia f tip
mancino/a left handed
mandare send
mandarino m tangerine
mandorla f almond
mangiare eat
manifesto m poster
maniglia f handle
mano f hand
manuale manual (adj)
manuale m manual (n)
manzo m beef
marca f brand (n)
marcia f gear
marcia indietro reverse gear
marciapiede m pavement, sidewalk
marcio/a rotten
mare m sea
Mare Baltico Baltic Sea
Mare del Nord m North Sea
marea f tide
marina f navy
marito m husband
marmellata f jam
marmellata d'arance marmalade
marmo m marble (n, stone)
marrone brown
martello m hammer
marzo m March
mascara m mascara
mascella f jaw
maschile male
massa f mass (volume)
materasso m mattress
matita f pencil
matrigna f stepmother
matrimonio m wedding
mattina f morning
mattone m brick
maturo/a ripe
mazza da golf golf club (stick)
mazzo m bunch (of flowers), pack (of cards)
meccanico m mechanic
medicina f medicine
medievale medieval
medio/a medium
mediocre average
mediterraneo Mediterranean
medusa f jellyfish
meglio better
melone m melon

ITALIAN → ENGLISH

meningite f meningitis
meno less
mensile monthly
menta f mint
mente f mind (n)
mentire lie (vb, fib)
mento m chin
mentre while
menu m menu
menù fisso set menu
menzionare mention (vb)
menzione f mention (n)
mercato m market
mercoledì m Wednesday
meringa f meringue
merluzzo m cod
meschino/a mean (adj, nasty)
mescolare mix
mese m month
Messa f mass (rel)
messaggio m message
metà f half
metallo m metal
metro m tape measure, metre
metropolitana f subway, metro
mettere put
mettere in contatto contact (vb)
mezzanotte midnight
mezzogiorno m midday, noon
mi me
Mi dispiace! Sorry!
Mi fa male It hurts
Mi sento male! I'm going to be sick!
miele m honey
miglio m mile
migliorare improve
mille m thousand
minestra f soup
ministro m minister (politics)
minuscolo/a tiny
minuto/a minute (adj, size)
minuto m minute (n, time)
miope short-sighted
mirtilli rossi redcurrants
miscuglio di frutta candita fruit mince
misterioso/a weird
misura f size, measure (n)
misurare measure (vb)
mobili mpl furniture
modulo m form
modulo registrazione registration form
moglie f wife
molla f spring (metal)
molletta da bucato clothes peg
molti many

molto lot
molto/a much, very
Molto lieto! How do you do?
Molto piacere! Pleased to meet you!
momento m moment
Monaco di Baviera Munich
monastero m monastery
mondo m world
moneta f coin
montagna f mountain
monumento m monument
morbido/a soft
morbillo m measles
mordere bite (vb)
morire die
morso m bite (n)
morte f death
morto/a dead
mosca f fly (n)
moschea f mosque
mostra f exhibition, show (n)
mostrare show (vb)
motocicletta f motorbike
motore m engine, motor
motoscafo m motorboat
mucca f cow
multa f fine (n)
multa per divieto di sosta parking ticket
municipio m town hall
muovere move
muro m wall
muscolo m muscle
museo m museum
musicista m/f musician
musulmano m Muslim
mutande f pants, underpants
mutandine f knickers, panties

N

nafta f diesel
narcotico m drug, narcotic
nascita f birth
nascondere hide
naso m nose
nastro m ribbon, tape
nastro adesivo m adhesive tape
Natale m Christmas
nato/a born
natura f nature
naturale natural
nausea f nausea
nave f boat, ship
navigare sail (vb)
navigazione f sailing
nazionale national
nazionalità f nationality

ITALIAN → ENGLISH

nè ... nè neither ... nor
nebbia f fog
necessario/a necessary
negativo/a negative
negozio m shop
negozio di bricolage DIY shop
negozio di ferramenta ironmonger's, hardware shop
negozio di macrobiotica health food shop
nel in
neozelandese m/f New Zealander
nero/a black
nessuno m nobody
neve f snow
nevica It is snowing
nido m nest, crèche
nient'altro nothing else
niente none, nothing
nipote f niece, granddaughter
nipote m nephew, grandson
no no
nocciole f hazelnuts
noce f nut, walnut
noce di cocco coconut
noi us, we
noioso/a boring
nome m name
nome di battesimo Christian name, first name
non not
non fumatori non-smoking
Non importa It doesn't matter
non potrei couldn't
non troppo cotto/a medium rare (meat)
nonna f grandmother
nonni grandparents
nonno m grandfather
nord m north
norvegese m/f Norwegian
Norvegia f Norway
nostalgia di casa homesickness
nostro/a our
nota f note
notizie fpl news
notte f night
novembre m November
nulla nothing
numero m number
numero telefonico m phone number
nuora f daughter-in-law
nuotare swim
Nuova Zelanda f New Zealand
nuovo/a new
nutrire feed (vb)
nuvola f cloud

O

o or
obbligatorio/a compulsory
oca f goose
occhiali m eyeglasses, spectacles, glasses
occhiali da sole sunglasses
occhiali di protezione goggles
occhio m eye
occupato/a busy, engaged, occupied
occupazione f occupation
oceano m ocean
odorare smell (vb)
odore m smell (n)
oggetti smarriti lost property
oggi m today
ogni each, every
ogni ora hourly
ogni tanto occasionally
ognuno everyone
olandese Dutch
oleoso/a greasy
olio m oil
olio di oliva olive oil
olio solare suntan oil
oliva f olive
oltre beyond
ombra f shade
ombrello m umbrella
ombretto m eye shadow
omelette f omelette
omosessuale gay
onda f wave
onesto/a honest
opera f opera
operatore turistico m tour operator
operazione f operation
opposto/a opposite
opuscolo m brochure
ora f hour, time
orario m timetable
orario d'apertura opening times
orario delle visite visiting hours
orchestra f orchestra
ordinare order (vb)
ordine m order (n)
orecchini earrings
orecchio m ear
orecchioni mpl mumps
organico/a organic (vegetables)
orlo m hem
ormeggio m mooring
oro m gold
orologio m clock, watch (n)
ospedale m hospital
ospitalità f hospitality
ospitare put up (guest)
ospite m/f visitor, guest
osso m bone
ostello m hostel
ostello della gioventù youth hostel

ITALIAN → ENGLISH

ottenere obtain
ottico m optician
ottobre m October
ovest m west

P

pacchetto m packet
pacco m package, parcel
pacemaker m pacemaker
padella f pan, frying pan
padiglione m ward (hospital)
padre m father
paese m country
Paesi Bassi Netherlands
pagamento m payment
pagare pay
pagato paid
pagina f page
pagine gialle Yellow Pages
paglia f straw
pagnotta f loaf
paio m pair
palazzo m palace
palestra f gym
paletta per la spazzatura dustpan
pallido/a pale
pallina f marble (n, toy)
palude f marsh
pancetta f bacon
panciotto m waistcoat
pane m bread
pane di segale f rye bread
pane integrale wholemeal bread
panfilo m yacht
panificio m bakery
panino m roll
panna f cream, breakdown (of car)
panna montata f whipped cream
pannolini usa e getta disposable diapers/ nappies
pannolino m diaper, nappy
pantaloni m trousers
pantofole f slippers
papavero m poppy
parabrezza windscreen
parafango m fender
parasole m sunshade
paraurti m bumper (car)
parcheggiare park (vb)
parchimetro m parking meter
parco m park (n)
parecchi several
parente m/f relative, relation
parenti acquisiti m in-laws

parlare speak, talk
parola f word
parolaccia f swear word
parole crociate crossword puzzle
parrucca f wig
parrucchiere/a m/f hairdresser
parte f part, share (n)
partenza f departure
particolari m details
particolarmente especially
partire depart
partita di calcio football match
partito m party (political)
Pasqua Easter
passaggio a livello level crossing
passaggio pedonale crossing, pedestrian crossing
passaporto m passport
passare pass (vb)
passato/a past
passeggero m passenger
passeggiata f walk (n)
passeggino m baby buggy, pushchair
passo m pass (n)
pasta f pastry
pasticceria f cake shop
pastiglie per la gola throat lozenges
pasto m meal
pastore m minister (church)
patata f potato
patatine fritte chips, crisps, French fries
patente f licence
patente di guida driving licence
patrigno m stepfather
pattinare skate (vb)
pattini da ghiaccio ice skates
pattino m skate (n)
patto m deal
pattumiera f dustbin, bin, waste bin
paura, paura di afraid, afraid of
pavimento m floor
paziente patient (adj)
paziente m/f patient (n)
pazzo/a mad
peccato pity
pecora f sheep
pedaggio toll
pedale m pedal
pedone m pedestrian
peggio/a worse
pelle f leather, skin
pelliccia f fur coat

pellicola f film
pelo m fur
penisola f peninsula
penna f pen
penna a sfera ballpoint pen
pensare think
pensionato m old-age pensioner
pensione f boarding house, guesthouse
pensione completa full board
pepe m pepper
per for, per
per esempio for example
per favore please
per la notte overnight
per lo più mostly
pera f pear
Perchè Why?
perchè because
percorso m way
perdere lose, leak (vb)
perdita f leak (n)
perduto/a lost
perfetto/a perfect
pericolo m danger
pericoloso/a dangerous
periodo m period
perla f pearl
permanente perm
permesso permit (n)
permesso di pesca fishing permit
permesso per caccia hunting permit
permettere allow, let, permit (vb)
pernottare stop over
persona f person
persone f people
pesante heavy
pesare weigh
pesca f peach
pesce m fish
pescivendolo m fishmonger's
peso m weight
pettine m comb
petto m chest
pezzi di ricambio car parts
pezzo m bit, piece
pezzo di ricambio spare part
piacere like (vb)
piangere cry
piano m piano, storey
pianta f plant (n), sole (foot)
pianta stradale street map
piantare plant (vb)
pianterreno m ground floor
piattino m saucer
piatto m dish, plate
piatto da asporto/ piatto da portar via take-away food
piazza f square (n)

picco m peak
piccolo/a small, little
picnic m picnic
piede m foot
piedi mpl feet
pieno/a full
pietra f stone
pigiama f pyjamas
pigro/a lazy
pila f flashlight
pillola f pill
pilota f pilot
pinne f flippers
pinze f pliers
pinzette f tweezers
pioggia f rain
piolo m peg
piolo da tenda tent peg
piombatura filling (tooth)
piombo m lead (n)
pipa f pipe
pirofilo/resistente al calore ovenproof
pirosi heartburn
piscina coperta/interna indoor pool
pisello m pea
pista di pattinaggio ice rink, skating rink
pista per biciclette cycle track
pista per principianti nursery slope
pista per sci ski slope
pistola f gun
pittura f paint (n)
pitturare paint (vb)
piu extra
più more
più tardi later
piumone m duvet
pizzo m lace (fabric)
plastica f plastic
pochi few
poco/a little
poco profondo shallow
polacco m Polish
polizia f police
poliziotto m policeman
pollice m inch, thumb
pollo m chicken
polmone m lung
Polonia f Poland
polso m wrist
poltrona f armchair
polvere f dust, powder
pomata f ointment
pomeriggio m afternoon
pomodoro m tomato
pompa f pump (n)
pompare pump (vb)
ponte m bridge
popolare popular
popolazione population
porcellana f china
porre place (vb)

porro m leek
porta f door
portabagagli m roof-rack, luggage rack, boot (car)
portachiavi m key ring
portafoglio m wallet
portare bring, carry, wear
portata principale main course
portiere m doorman, porter
portinaio/a m/f janitor
porto m port, harbour
Portogallo m Portugal
portoghese m/f Portuguese
porzione f portion
posare place (vb)
posate cutlery
possibile possible
posta f post, mail (n)
posta aerea f airmail
posta raccomandata registered mail
posteggio per taxi taxi rank
postino/a m/f postman/woman
posto m place (n)
posto al finestrino window seat
posto sul corridoio aisle seat
posto vacante vacancy
postumi di una sbornia hangover
potere can (vb, be able to), may, might
potrei could
povero/a poor (impoverished)
pozza f pool
pranzo m lunch
pratica f practice
praticare practise
preciso/a accurate
preferire prefer
preferito/a favourite
prefisso m dialling code
pregare pray
premio m prize
prendere take, catch
prendere a calci kick (vb)
prendere a prestito borrow
prendere un biglietto per book (vb, ticket)
prenotazione f reservation (seats)
preoccupato/a worried
presa di corrente socket
presentare introduce, present (vb)
presente present (adj)
preservativo m condom
pressappoco roughly

pressione f pressure
pressione alta del sangue high blood pressure
pressione del sangue blood pressure
pressione delle gomme tyre pressure
prestare lend
presto soon, quickly
prete m priest
previsioni del tempo weather forecast
prezzo m price
prigione f **prison**
prima classe first class
prima colazione breakfast
prima di before
primavera f spring (season)
primo/a first
Primo Ministro m prime minister
primo piano first floor
principale main
principiante beginner
privato/a private
privo di sensi unconscious
probabilmente probably
problema m problem
profondo/a deep
profumo m perfume
programma m programme, program
proibito forbidden
prolunga extension lead
prolungamento m extension
promessa f promise
pronto ready
pronto soccorso m casualty department, first aid
pronunciare pronounce
proprietaria f landlady
proprietario m landlord, owner
proprio just (only)
prosciutto m ham
prossima settimana next week
prossimo/a next
protestante Protestant
provare try
provarsi try on
prugna f plum
prurito m itch (n)
pubblicità f advert, advertisement
pubblico/a public
pubblico m audience
pulce f flea
pulito/a clean
pungere sting (vb)
puntine f points (car)

punto m point (n), stitch
puntura f sting (n)
puntura di insetto m insect bite
purè di patate mashed potatoes

Q

qua here
quadrante m dial (n)
quadrato/a square (adj, shape)
quadro m painting (picture)
qualche some
qualche cosa anything
qualche volta sometimes
qualcosa something, anything
qualcuno m someone, somebody
Quale? Which?
qualità f quality
Quando? When?
Quanti? How many?
quantità f amount, quantity
Quanto costa questo? How much is it?
Quanto le devo? How much do I owe you?
quarantena f quarantine
quarto m quarter
quasi almost, nearly
quegli m those
quei those
quel that
quelli those
quello that
quercia f oak
questa sera f tonight
questa settimana this week
questo/a this
qui here, over here
quindicina f fortnight
quota d'entrata admission fee, entrance fee

R

rabbia f rabies
racchetta f racket
racchetta da tennis tennis racket
raccolta f harvest
raccomandare recommend
raccordo m junction
radere shave
radiatore m radiator
radio f radio
raffreddore da fieno hay fever
ragazza f girl, girlfriend
ragazzo m boy, boyfriend
raggi-X m X-ray

raggio m spoke
ragionevole reasonable
ragnatela f web
ragno m spider
rana f frog
rapportare report (vb)
rapporto m report (n)
rappresentante m sales representative
raro/a rare
rasoio m razor
rastrello m rake
rattura f tear (n)
ravanello m radish
razza f race (people)
re m king
reale royal
realizzare realize
recentemente recently
recinto m fence
regalo m gift, present
regalo di nozze wedding present
regalo per il compleanno birthday present
reggiseno m bra
regina f queen
regione f district, region
registrare register, record (vb)
registratore m tape recorder
registro m register (n)
Regno Unito m U.K.
regolo m ruler (for measuring)
remare row (vb)
remo m oar
rene m kidney
Repubblica Ceca Czech Republic
residente m/f resident
respirare breathe
respiratore m snorkel
restare remain
restituire give back
resto m rest (n, remainder)
restringersi shrink
rete f net
reumatismo m rheumatism
riagganciare hang up (phone)
ribes neri blackcurrants
ricaricare recharge
riccio/a curly
ricco/a rich
ricetta f prescription, recipe
ricevere get
ricevitore m receiver
ricevuta f receipt
ricezione f reception
richiedere require, request (vb)
richiesta f request (n)
riconoscere recognize

ITALIAN → ENGLISH

ricordare remember
ricordo souvenir m souvenir
ridere laugh (vb)
ridicolo/a ridiculous
ridurre reduce
riduzione f reduction
riempire fill
riempirsi fill up
rifiutare refuse (vb)
rifiuti mpl litter (n)
rimandare postpone
rimanere stay
rimborsare refund (vb)
rimborso m refund (n)
rimorchiare tow
rimorchio m trailer
ringraziare thank
riparare mend, repair (vb)
riparazione f repair (n)
ripetere repeat
ripido/a steep
ripieno m stuffed
riposare rest (vb)
riposo rest (n, relaxation)
risata f laugh (n)
riscaldamento heating
riscaldamento centrale central heating
riserva f reserve
riserva naturale f nature reserve
riso m rice
rispondere answer, reply (vb)
risposta f answer, reply (n)
ritardare delay (vb)
ritardo/a late
ritardo m delay (n)
ritirato/a sheltered
ritiro bagagli baggage reclaim
ritornare return (vb), come back, go back
ritorno m return (n)
ritratto m portrait
riva f shore
rivista f magazine
rivoltante revolting
roccia f rock
romanzo m novel
rompere break, tear (vb)
rosa pink
rosa f rose
rosolia f German measles, rubella
rossetto m lipstick
rosso red
rosso per le guancie blusher
rotolo m coil
rotondo/a round
rotto/a broken
rovesciare knock over, spill
rovina f ruin (n)
rovinare ruin (vb), spoil
rubare steal

rubato stolen
rughe f wrinkles
rullino a colori colour film
rum m rum
rumore m noise, row (n)
rumoroso/a noisy
ruota f wheel
ruota di scorta spare tyre/wheel
ruscello m stream
russare snore
ruvido/a rough

S

sabato Saturday
sabbia f sand
sacchetto di plastica plastic bag
sacco a pelo m sleeping bag
sala f hall
sala d'aspetto waiting room
sala da pranzo dining room
sala delle partenze departure lounge
sala di prova f fitting room
salario m wage
salato/a savoury
sale m salt
salire get on, climb
salmone m salmon
salmone affumicato smoked salmon
salotto m lounge
salsa f sauce
salsiccia f sausage
saltare jump
Salute! cheers!
saluto m greeting
salvagente m life belt
salvamento m rescue (n)
salvare rescue (vb), save
sandali mpl sandals
sangue m blood
sanguinare bleed
sano/a healthy
santo/a holy
sapere know
sapone m soap
sapore m flavour
saporito savoury
sarto m tailor
sbagliato/a wrong
sbaglio m mistake
sbucciare peel (vb)
scacchi m chess
scadente cheap
scadere expire
scaffale m shelf
scala f ladder
scala mobile escalator
scalare climb
scale f stairs
scambiare exchange
scandente poor (quality)
scarafaggio m cockroach

scarpa f shoe
scarponi da sci ski boot
scarto m waste (n)
scatola f box, can
scatola dei fusibili fuse box
scatola di cartone carton
scegliere choose
scenario m scenery
scendere get off
scheda telefonica f phone card
scheggia f splinter
schermo m screen
scherzo m joke
schiantare crash (vb)
schiena f back
sci m ski (n)
sci acquatico waterskiing
sciare ski (vb)
sciarpa f scarf
sciocco/a silly
sciogliere melt
sciopero m strike
sciroppo per la tosse cough mixture
scivolare slide, slip (vb)
scivolata f slip (n)
scivolo m slide (n)
scivoloso slippery
scodella f bowl
scogliera f cliff
scola pasta f colander
scommessa bet (n)
scommettere bet (vb)
scomodo/a inconvenient, uncomfortable
scomparire disappear
scompartimento m compartment
sconto m discount
sconto per studenti student discount
scopa f broom
scoppiare burst
scoprire discover
scorciatoia f short-cut
scorrevole fluent
scorsa settimana last week
scorta f stock
scottatura f sunburn
Scozia f Scotland
scozzese m/f Scot, Scottish (n, adj)
scrivere write
scuola f school
scuola materna f nursery school
scuotere shake
scuro/a dark
scusa f apology
scusi excuse me
Scusi? Pardon?
sdraiarsi lie down
se if
sebbene although
secchio m bucket, pail

secolo m century
seconda classe second class
secondo/a second (adj, number)
secondo m second (n, of time)
sedano m celery
sedere sit
sedia f chair, seat
sedia a rotelle wheelchair
sedia a sdraio deck chair
seggiolino per macchina child car seat
seggiolone m high chair
seggiovia f chair lift
segnale stradale f signpost
segnale m signal
segnale di linea libera dialling tone
segnale stradale road sign
segno m sign (n)
segretario m secretary
seguire follow
self service self-service
sella f saddle
semaforo m traffic light
seminterrato m basement
semplice plain, simple
sempre always
senape f mustard
seno m breast
senso unico one-way street
sentenza f sentence (law)
sentiero m lane, path, footpath
sentire feel, hear
senza without
senza reggiseno topless
senza zucchero sugar-free
separare separate (vb)
separato/a separate (adj)
sera f evening
serbatoio m tank
serio/a serious
serpente m snake
serranda f shutter
serratura f lock (n)
serratura automatica central locking
servizio m service, service charge
sesso m sex (gender)
seta f silk
setaccio m sieve
settembre m September

ITALIAN → ENGLISH

settico/a septic
settimana week
settimanale weekly
sezione department
sfuggire escape (vb)
shampoo e messa in piega shampoo and set
si yes
sicuramente definitely
sicuro/a sure, safe
sidro m cider
sigaretta f cigarette
sigaro m cigar
Signor m Mr
signora f lady
Signora f, signorina f Mrs/Ms
signorina Miss
silenzio m silence
simile similar, like (adj)
sinagoga f synagogue
sinistra left
sistemare arrange
slitta f sledge
slogare sprain (vb)
smalto per unghie m nail varnish/polish
sobborgo m suburb
sobrio/a sober
soccorso alpino mountain rescue
socio m partner (business)
soda f soda
soffitta f attic
soffitto m ceiling
soggiorno m living room
sogliola f sole (fish)
soldi m money
sole m sun
sollevare lift (vb)
solo alone, only, single
solubile soluble
soluzione per lenti a contatto soaking solution
sonnifero m sleeping pill
sono are, am
sopra above, over, on
sordo/a deaf
sorella f sister
sorgente calda hot spring
sorpassare overtake
sorridere smile (vb)
sorriso m smile (n)
sorta f kind (n)
sospensione f suspension
sostituto di fianco hip replacement
sottile thin
sotto below, under
sottosopra upside down
sottoterra underground
sottotitolo m subtitle

sovrano m ruler (sovereign)
Spagna f Spain
spagnoli/e m/f Spanish
spagnolo/a m/f Spaniard
spalla f shoulder
spazzatura f trash
spazzola f brush
spazzola per capelli hairbrush
spazzolino da denti toothbrush
spazzolino da unghie m nail brush
spazzolino per le unghie scrubbing brush
specchietto retrovisore rear-view mirror
specchio m mirror
specialità speciality
specie f sort (n)
spegnere turn off, switch off
spendere spend
spento off
speranza f hope (n)
sperare hope (vb)
spese fpl expenses
spesso often
spesso/a thick
spettacolo burattini m puppet show
spezia f spice
spiaggia f beach, seaside
spiaggia per nudisti nudist beach
spiccioli mpl change (n, coins)
spiegare explain
spilla f brooch
spillo m pin
spillo di sicurezza m safety pin
spina f plug (elec), thorn
spina dorsale f spine
spinaci m spinach
spingere push
spirito m spirits
splendere shine
spogliatoio m changing room (for sports)
sporco/a dirty
sportello automatico auto-teller, cash dispenser
sposa f bride
sposato/a married
sposo m bridegroom
sprecare waste (vb)
spugna f sponge
spuntato/a blunt
spuntino m snack
squadra f team
staccato/a disconnected
stadio m stadium
stagione f season
stagnola f tinfoil

stamattina this morning
stampa f print (n)
stampare print (vb)
stampe printed matter
stampella f coat hanger
stampelle f crutches
stanco/a tired
stantio/a stale
stanza ammobiliata furnished
stanza dei bambini nursery
starnutire sneeze (vb)
starnuto m sneeze (n)
stasera tonight
Stati Uniti (d'America) United States
statua f statue
stazione f station
stazione di servizio petrol station
stazione ferroviaria railway station
stazione termale f spa
stella f star (sky)
sterlina f pound (money)
sterzare steer
stesso/a same
stitico/a constipated
stivale m boot (shoe)
stivali boots
stoffa f material
stomaco m stomach
stomatite mouth ulcer
storia f history
storico/a historic
stoviglie f crockery
straccio m rag
straccio per pavimento floorcloth
stracotto overdone
strada f road, street
strada a pedaggio toll road
strada principale main road
straniero/a foreign
straniero m foreigner
strano/a odd, peculiar, strange
straordinario/a extraordinary
strato di ghiaccio invisibile black ice
stretto/a narrow, tight
strofinaccio m dishtowel, duster
studente m student
stufa heater
stufato m stew
stupefacente astonishing
stupido/a stupid
stuzzicadente toothpick
su on, up
subito straightaway
succedere happen
succhiotto m dummy

succo m juice
succo d'arancia orange juice
succo di frutta fruit juice
succo di pomodoro tomato juice
succursale f branch (office)
sud m south
Sudafrica f South Africa
sudafricano/a m/f South African (adj, n)
sudare sweat (vb)
sudicio/a filthy
sudore m sweat (n)
sugo di carne gravy
suocera f mother-in-law
suoceri m parents-in-law
suocero m father-in-law
suola f sole (shoe)
suolo m ground
suonare ring (vb)
supplemento m supplement
surriscaldare overheat
svedese m/f Swede, Swedish (n, adj)
svegliarsi wake up
sveglio awake
svenire faint (vb)
Svezia f Sweden
sviluppare develop, film processing
svitare unscrew
Svizzera f Switzerland
svizzero/a m/f Swiss
svizzero/a tedesco/a m/f Swiss-German

T

tabellone noticeboard
tacchino m turkey
tacco m heel (shoe)
taccuino m notebook
tachimetro m speedometer
tagliare (a pezzi) chop, cut (vb)
tagliente sharp
taglio m cut (n)
taglio di capelli haircut
talco m talcum powder
tallone m heel (foot)
tampone m tampon
tappeto m carpet, rug
tappo m cork, top, plug (bath)
tardi late
targa f number plate, registration number
tariffa f fare
tariffa economica cheap rate
tariffa massima f peak rate
tasca f pocket
tassa f tax

tassì m cab, taxi
tassista m/f taxi driver
tasso m rate (of exchange)
tavola da surf surfboard
tavoletta di cioccolato bar of chocolate
tavolo m table
taxi m cab, taxi
tazza f cup
tè tea
teatro m theatre
tedesco/a m/f German (adj, n)
teiera f teapot
telefonare a carico del destinatario collect call
telefonata f phone call
telefono m phone, telephone
telefono cellulare mobile phone
telefono pubblico m payphone
televisione f television
temperatura f temperature
tempesta f storm
tempia f temple (anat)
tempio m temple (rel)
tempo m weather
temporale m thunderstorm
temporaneo/a temporary
tenda f curtain, tent
tenda veneziana f blind (n, for window)
tendine m tendon
tenere keep, hold
Tenga il resto! Keep the change!
tennis m tennis
tergicristallo m windscreen wiper
terminale terminal
termometro m thermometer
termosifone heater
terra f earth, land, ground
terremoto m earthquake
terrlblle dreadful
tessuto m cloth
tessuto sintetico man-made fibre
testa f head
testimone m/f witness
tettarella f teat
tetto m roof
tettuccio apribile sunroof
timido/a shy
timone m rudder
tintoria dry cleaner's
tintura f dye
tipico/a typical
tipo m type

tirare pull
tirare diritto straight on
tisana f herbal tea
toilette toilet
toilette per donne ladies' toilet
toilette per uomini gents' toilet
tonno m tuna
tonsillite f tonsillitis
topo m mouse, rat
torcia f torch
torre f tower
torta f cake, pie
tosse f cough (n)
tossire cough (vb)
totale m total
tovaglia f tablecloth
tovaglioli di carta paper napkins
tovagliolo m napkin
tra among
tradurre translate
traduttore m translator
traduzione f translation
traffico m traffic
traghetto m ferry, car ferry
tram m tram
tramezzino m sandwich
tramonto m sunset
trampolino m diving board
trampolino per sci ski jump
tranquillante m tranquillizer
tranquillo/a quiet
trapano m drill (n)
trapunta f quilt
treccia f plait
treno m train
triste sad
tromba f horn (car)
trota f trout
trovare find
tu you
tubo di scappamento m exhaust pipe
tubo di scarico drain
tubo flessibile hose pipe
tuffarsi dive (vb)
tuono m thunder
tuorlo m yolk
turchese turquoise
Turchia f Turkey
turco/a m/f Turk, Turkish (n, adj)
tuta da ginnastica f tracksuit
tutti e due both
tutto everything
tutto/a whole

U

ubriaco/a drunk
uccello m bird
uccidere kill
UE f EU

ufficio m office
ufficio informazioni enquiry desk
ufficio postale post office
uguale even
ulcera f ulcer
ulteriore further
ultimo/a last
ultimo piano top floor
umido/a damp, humid
umorismo m humour
un altro another
una scatola di cioccolatini chocolates (box of)
una settimana fa a week ago
una volta f once
ungherese m/f Hungarian (adj, n)
Ungheria f Hungary
unghia f nail
unire join
università university
uno, una one
untuoso/a greasy
uomini m men
uomo m man
uova strapazzate scrambled eggs
uovo m egg
uovo di Pasqua Easter egg
uovo in camicia poached egg
urgente urgent
usanza f custom
usare use
usato second-hand, used
uscita f exit
uscita di sicurezza emergency exit, fire exit
usuale, di solito usual, usually
utensili da cucina cooking utensils
utile useful
uva grape
uva passa raisin

V

va bene all right, okay
vacanza f holiday, vacation
vacanza organizzata package holiday
vacanze holidays
vaccinazione f vaccination
vaglia postale money order
vagone m coach (railway)
vagone letto sleeping car
vagone ristorante buffet car
valanga f avalanche
valido/a valid

valigia f case, suitcase
valle f valley
valore m worth, value (n)
valuta f currency
valutare value (vb)
valvola f valve
vanga f spade
vaniglia f vanilla
vapore m steam
varicella f chicken pox
vassoio m tray
vecchio/a old
vedere see
vedova f vedovo m widow, widower
vegetariano m vegetarian
veicolo m vehicle
veicolo a trazione a 4 ruote four-wheel-drive vehicle
vela f sail (n)
veleno m poison
velenoso/a poisonous
veloce fast
velocità f speed
vena f vein
vendere sell
vendita f sale
venditore m salesperson
venerdì Friday
Venerdì Santo Good Friday
venire come
venire a prendere fetch
ventilatore m fan
vento m wind
ventoso/a windy
verde green
verdure f vegetables
vergogna f shame
verificare check (vb)
verme m maggot
vero/a real, true
versare pour
vertiginoso/a dizzy
vescica f blister
vespa f wasp
vestaglia f dressing gown
vestiti m clothes
vestito m dress, suit
veterinario m vet (veterinarian)
vetrina f shop window
via via, by, away
viaggiare travel
viaggio m journey
viaggio d'affari business trip
viaggio in nave boat trip
viale m avenue
vicino/a m/f neighbour
vicino near, nearby
Vienna f Vienna
vietato prohibited
vigili del fuoco fire brigade
Vigilia di Capodanno New Year's Eve
Vigilia di Natale Christmas Eve

vigneto m vineyard
villaggio m village
vincere win
vino m wine
vino amabile medium dry (wine)
vino da tavola table wine
vino di casa house wine
Vino di Oporto m port (wine)
vino rosso m red wine
viola purple
violazione f rape (n)
violentare rape (vb)
violetto f violet
virus m virus
visita f visit (n)
visitare visit (vb)
vista f sight, view
visto m visa
vita f life, waist
vite f screw (n)
vitello m veal, calf
vivace lively
vivere live
voce f voice
voi you
volante steering wheel
volantino m leaflet
volare fly (vb)
volere want
volo m flight
volo charter charter flight
volo coincidenza connecting flight
volpe f fox
voltaggio m voltage
vomitare vomit
vulcano m volcano
vuoto/a empty

Z

zaino m backpack
zanzara f mosquito
zero m zero
zia f aunt
zio m uncle
zona f zone
zoo m zoo
zucchero m sugar